OTHER BOOKS BY RAY AND ANNE ORTLUND

Be a New Christian All Your Life, Fleming H. Revell (for new Christians or those who want to be renewed)

Building a Great Marriage, Fleming H. Revell (for any age but especially early marriage)

Children Are Wet Cement, Fleming H. Revell (handling children; Christy Award for best marriage-family book of 1982)

Confident in Christ, Multnomah (what it means to be in Christ; its privileges, its responsibilities)

Disciplines of the Beautiful Woman, Word Publishing (life management through a notebook, desk, wardrobe, etc.)

Disciplines of the Heart, Word Publishing (on a woman's inner life)

Disciplines of the Home, Word Publishing (on family life together)

Discipling One Another, Word Publishing (how-to's for small groups)

Fix Your Eyes on Jesus, Word Publishing (practical ways to stay Christ-centered)

Joanna: A Story of Renewal, Word Publishing (Anne's first fiction—to teach spiritual renewal)

Lord, Make My Life a Miracle, Regal Books (priorities to live by)

My Sacrifice, His Fire, Word Publishing (daily devotional readings for women)

Three Priorities for a Strong Local Church, Word Publishing (for pastors and lay leaders)

Up with Worship, Regal Books (what should happen between your ears on a Sunday morning)

You Don't Have to Quit, Oliver-Nelson (perseverance in marriage, job, school, relationships, etc.)

A MAN AND HIS LOVES

RAY AND ANNE ORTLUND

WORD PUBLISHING
Dallas•London•Vancouver•Melbourne

A MAN AND HIS LOVES

Unless otherwise indicated, Scripture quotations used in this book are from the Holy Bible, New International Version, copyright © 1973, 1978, 1984 by the New York International Bible Society. Used by permission of Zondervan Bible Publishers.

Those indicated KJV are from the King James Version of the Bible.

Those indicated PHILLIPS are from J. B. Phillips: The New Testament in Modern English. Revised Edition. Copyright © J. B. Phillips, 1958, 1960, 1972. Used by permission of Macmillan Publishing Co., Inc.

Those indicated RSV are from the Revised Standard Version of the Bible. Copyright © 1946, 1952, 1971, 1973 by the Division of Christian Education of the National Council of the Churches of Christ in the USA. Used by permission.

Those indicated TEV are from Today's English Version (The Good News Bible), Old Testament © 1976 by the American Bible Society; New Testament © 1966, 1971, 1976, American Bible Society. Used by permission.

Those indicated TLB are from The Living Bible (Wheaton, Illinois: Tyndale House Publishers, 1971), and are used by permission.

Library of Congress Cataloging-in-Publication Data

Ortlund, Raymond C.
    A man and his loves / Ray and Anne Ortlund.
      p. cm.
    ISBN 0-8499-1069-2
    1. Men—Religious life. 2. Christian life—1960– 3. Love—Religious aspects—Christianity. I. Ortlund, Anne. II. Title.
BV4528.2.O77   1994
248.8'42—dc20   93–47504
                                                CIP

Printed in the United States of America

4 5 6 7 8 9 LB 9 8 7 6 5 4 3 2 1

Dedicated to the memory of our fathers,
Ben Ortlund and Joe Sweet,
who transmitted to us not only life
but life in Christ

Contents

Foreword

And God saw everything that he had made,
and, behold, it was very good.
—Genesis 1:31, KJV

God made manhood, and it is very good. Being a man is a God-given privilege. So when the world sneers at manhood, we men have something to say in reply. *God* made manhood, and it is *very good.*

Moreover, God did not make us men to be loners. In fact, the Garden of Eden was perfect except for this one thing: "It is not good that the man should be alone," God said in Genesis 2:18 (KJV). Manhood in isolation was never right. From the beginning, a true man was to give himself away in bold, loving initiative toward others.

My dad and mom have written this book to help us men find our way back to the Creator's intention for true manhood. And after years of widespread confusion about and even hostility toward manhood in our society, many men are yearning to hear God's message.

Let me tell you something about my dad. He is real. The man you hear on "The Haven of Rest" radio program, the man whose books you read, the man whom you see preaching in significant pulpits—he is real, he is genuine, he is credible. There is not one public figure and another, different private figure. There is only one Ray Ortlund, Sr. As his son, I know. I have seen him up close. And I respect my father more than I respect any other man on the face of the earth. This man can be trusted.

And here is something about my mom. She is a highly talented woman of drive and conviction, but she does not compete with my father. She does not elbow her way into the limelight. She is too wise and too secure in God to fall prey to stylish feminist hysteria. My mother gladly supports and affirms my father. And in doing so, she displays a warmth, and a magnetism, and a dignity that the strident champions of exaggerated feminist entitlements have never known. She is a classical woman. She can be listened to.

As you read this book, open your heart to God. Ask Him to speak to you. Give Him access to your secret hypocrisies that keep you from true, God-honoring manhood. Perhaps you have never exposed them to Him before. But remember that He does not despise you. He loves you and can make you into a man worthy of the name. Let this be the start of a new era in your life. Do not let your past define your future. Let the mercy of God define your future. And use this book to seek God for a fresh start now.

Some of the biblical principles you will read in this book will challenge you. They may even seem out of reach. (The life of obedience is not for those who fear heights.) But let this sink in: Along with many others, my dad is himself a living embodiment of the things he teaches here. It is possible, in the mercy of God, to become the kind of man described in this book. Take it one step at a time. Draw strength from God. And go for it!

> To thee, O Lord, I lift up my soul.
> O my God, in thee I trust,
> > let me not be put to shame,
> > let not my enemies exult over me. . . .
> Make me to know thy ways, O Lord;
> > teach me thy paths.
> Lead me in thy truth, and teach me,
> > for thou art the God of my salvation;
> > for thee I wait all the day long (Ps. 25:1–2, 4–5, RSV).

—Raymond C. Ortlund, Jr., Ph.D.
Trinity Evangelical Divinity School
September 22, 1993

A fellow athletic club member, talking recently to Ray:
> "You still writing books?"
> "Yep."
> "What's the new one on?"
> "Well, it's about a man and his loves."
> "Oh, like toys—sports cars and so on?"
> "No, his relationships!"
> "Oh . . . You started down on the list."

A typical guy, quoted in *The Friendless American Male:*
> "Of course I don't have friends; I'm a man! My wife is the one with friends."[1]

And yet Jesus tells us,
> "You must love the Lord your God with all your heart, and with all your soul, and with all your strength, and with all your mind. And you must love your neighbor just as much as you love yourself" (Luke 10:27, TLB).

Let's talk about how a real man can learn to love.

---

1. David W. Smith (Ventura, CA: Regal Books, 1983), 50.

PART I

Your Love for Being a Man

1 The real masculine thing

Ray writes . . .

What does "manly" mean? What's "masculine"?

Tattoos, Harleys, headbands?

Neck chains tangled in your chest hair?

Is "manly" when your pocket knife doubles as a toothpick, you have grease under your toenails, and you've totaled every car you've ever owned? Is all that the real masculine thing?

No.

Or you wear short shorts, a tank top, sandals and styled hair?

And you know every technique for stretching before you work out, and you have taboule and skinless chicken with your beer?

And you moonlight, you finagle for deals, your bank account suddenly doubles and nobody knows it but you and the bank? Is all that the real masculine thing?

No.

Listen to what the Bible says being a male is all about:

1. You were made in the image of God (Gen. 1:26).
   Awesome.

2. You were appointed ruler over the whole created world (Gen. 1:26), obviously with tremendous intellectual and administrative powers.

3. You were made out of dirt (Gen. 2:7)! That's so you won't get heady.

4. You were immediately given a job (Gen. 2:15). A job gives you a sense of identification, achievement, and contribution.

5. You were incomplete without a woman (Gen. 2:18–22). If you're single, still appreciate women, be influenced by them. If you're married, hold your woman tight—that's what "cleave" means (Gen. 2:24, KJV).

6. You were touched with the magic power to reproduce (Gen. 4:1).

7. And, in God's image, you were made a creator, too. Adam's descendants immediately began building cities and making music and forging bronze and iron (Gen. 4:17–22) . . . and microchips and space rockets . . . The list goes on and on. He couldn't have done it without woman . . .

But this book is about the man. Let's talk about how rich your life can be as you walk with God, how full of fun and dignity and meaning. And let's talk about the significance of all your personal connections.

God has created you for a purpose—to take you up into His own magnificent purposes! And if you'll go along with Him—more and more,

> Your sincerity will become your success;
> Your goodness will become your glory;
> Your self-control will become your strength;
> And your holiness will become your honor.

2 Coming back together

Ray again . . .

Does the average guy *plan it out in advance* to be passive, inexpressive, unresponsive? Does he think that's cool? What do you think?

I was preaching a while back from Ezekiel 37, about God's telling Ezekiel in a vision to preach to a whole valley full of dismembered skeletons lying around, "dry bones."

In the middle of it all, I became aware of the male faces in front of me.

Blank.

Dull.

Bored.

I thought, "My cow, I'm another Ezekiel! I'm preaching to dry bones."

Does the average guy in church just *expect* to check out? Look, I'm a man, too. I'm not angry at men. But I'm aroused over the state many of us have fallen into.

Whenever Anne and I go to a small midwestern town to hold a conference, I ask the pastor to take me to the local coffee shop

5

about ten in the morning. I know what's going to happen; the scene is almost always the same.

The men come out of their fields or shops and amble in. They slap down their caps or hats on a table, toss a quarter into a mug somewhere, and pour themselves a cup of coffee. Then they gather around tables or counters.

What do they talk about? Worries about one of their kids? Hurts over a fight with the wife? Concerns about their family finances? No way; that would be woman-talk. Although these anxieties may be just under the surface, they probably don't even discuss them much at home.

No, they talk about taxes. The stupid government. Their ball team's lousy coach who blew the last game.

And the guy who spouts the most negatives, wins.

Why do so many men seem to suppress their true feelings and needs? Why do they seem "out of it" with people, dull and bland with God? Why this restricting of joy and enthusiasm for life?

Maybe it's their embarrassment and insecurity these days simply over being men. You've probably read comments like this one:

> *The male is in crisis.* Buffeted by the women's movement, constrained by a traditional and internationalized definition of "masculinity," men literally don't know who they are, what women want from them, or even what they want from themselves.[1]

And we seem, right now, to be trying so hard to emphasize the equality between men and women that we're clouding the uniqueness of each. The fact is, we're equal but different. And *vive la différence!*

Well, let's go back to Jesus Himself as the model Man. He's certainly somebody ordinary workmen can relate to—this blue-collar carpenter, planing, sawing, and hammering at His bench.

---

1. James Levine, "What Makes a Man?" *Psychology Today,* November 1979, 147.

But intellectuals and leaders are attracted, too. He was a thinker and a forceful communicator.

And body-builders and psychologists alike have got to be awed: He walked at least 2,500 miles in His three-year ministry, usually surrounded by crowds, constantly preaching and healing, and always aware of being despised and plotted against.

In this setting He laughed, He wept. He whipped money-changers out of His temple. He cuddled children. He cherished best friends, both men and women. *He loved intensely.*

God "became flesh and lived for a while among us" (John 1:4). He was well-rounded, full-orbed. He was meek but not weak, vulnerable but never a wimp.

When you look at Jesus a principle becomes clear:

> You see that righteousness produces courage and strength, but sin buckles a man's knees and cuts him down to cowardice.

That's the simple difference:

> The wicked man flees though no one pursues,
>   but the righteous [made righteous in Christ]
>   are bold as a lion (Prov. 28:1).

This principle—that sin makes wimps and righteousness makes strong men—explains God's word to Joshua, one of His greatest generals:

> Be strong and very courageous. Be careful to obey all the [Scripture]. . . . Do not let this Book of the Law depart from your mouth; meditate on it day and night. . . . Then you will be prosperous and successful.
>
> Have I not commanded you? Be strong and courageous (Josh. 1:7–9).

The connection's clear: Stay in the Book and you stay right-eous; stay righteous and you stay strong.

What's happened in the last few years? We men got distracted and let our women become the only Bible students. The inevitable result is that we've been losing both our righteousness and our strength.

Maybe, though, we're starting to change.

Maybe we're concluding that being wimps is a bummer. (Shifting from offense to defense hasn't been fun.)

And maybe meism is losing its appeal. We're disillusioned over the material greed of the eighties. We're disappointed with the anemic emptiness of the privacy and autonomy which we once hungered after. We're tired of mask-wearing, of strutting, of hurting with no one to comfort us, of losing with no one to lift us up, of winning with no one to share our victories.

The personal ads, the singles bars, the dating clubs all reveal how it's been with us recently: Morally we've gone belly up.

Says Gordon Dalbey,

> Certainly we men do not fantasize before *Playboy* centerfolds because we are so courageous before real-live, three-dimensional women, but rather, because we fear them; we do not beat up women because we are so strong, but rather, because we feel so powerless before them; we do not impregnate women and leave them to consider an abortion because we are so self-reliant, but rather, because we feel so inadequate to be responsible fathers and husbands.[2]

The time has come, not to sneak off to the woods and beat drums but to "beat our breasts" in repentance and look again for God's way. Remember, it's our sin which has cut us down to wimp-size.

Maybe we're finally ready.

Maybe *you're* ready.

But how do you change—and to what?

Larry Crabb says trying to change all by yourself in a lonely, solo project is like a paralytic trying to stand up, or a lung cancer

---

2. *Healing the Masculine Soul* (Dallas: Word Publishing, 1988), 21.

patient trying not to cough.[3] We've been ailing too long in our
self-inflicted macho independence and loneliness.

We need a grand together-move back to love, back to those
two great commandments: to love God with all our hearts, souls,
strength, and minds, and to love others as ourselves. And I have
a hunch that's what we men are secretly starting to long for.

Then we need to get together—in small groups and large—
and help each other do it.

> Let us consider how we may spur one another on
> toward love. . . . Let us encourage one another (Heb.
> 10:24, 25).

You say that's for women, that men aren't made for all this
reach-out-and-touch-someone stuff? Well, that's the current,
widely believed myth: "Men don't do that, men aren't like that,
men are different. . . ."

Baloney. God made men to love. He didn't design His two
great commandments just for women.

Old Testament David often directed outnumbered armies to
tremendous victories in battle, and he personally clubbed to death
both lions and bears that attacked his sheep. But when his dear
friend Jonathan was killed, David lamented,

> I grieve for you, Jonathan my brother;
>   you were very dear to me.
> Your love for me was wonderful,
>   more wonderful than that of women (2 Sam. 1:26).

First-century Saul ruthlessly tracked down Christians, both
men and women, and shoved them into prisons. But after his
conversion—listen to him:

> We loved you so much that we were delighted to
> share with you not only the gospel of God but our lives

---

3. *Men and Women: Enjoying the Difference* (Grand Rapids: Zondervan,
1991), 100.

as well, because you had become so dear to us (1 Thess. 2:8).

Hear what God is wanting to tell you, not through the words of sensitive John but through big, rough Peter the fisherman:

> Though you have not seen [God], . . . love him.
> And have sincere love for your brothers; love one another deeply, from the heart (1 Pet. 1:8, 22).

Loving God, loving others—have those loves been weak or missing in your own life?

I think guys are ready for a Spirit-empowered move back to love.

Old Testament men and boys came together three times a year in huge, male-only conventions—kind of like the current Promise Keepers—"to appear before the Sovereign Lord, the God of Israel" (Exod. 34:23). I'll bet it was a heck of a lot of fun. The old cliché is still right: When coals separate they cool off; to stay hot they have to get together.

Most of us men have too long been spiritually and emotionally separated; we've been dry bones—scattered, dismembered skeletons.

Coals that have cooled.

Joyless. Passive. Bland.

But in Ezekiel 37, when these dry bones "heard the word of the Lord," what happened?

> There was a noise, a rattling sound, and the bones came together, bone to bone. . . .
> And breath entered them, and they came to life and stood up on their feet—a vast army (Ezek. 37:7, 10). Unified! Powerful!

Hold it.

Is it just me, or do you hear a rattling sound?

3 No whining, no alibis

Ray again . . .

I have a conviction that many men don't bond well with their wives—or with anyone else—because they haven't bonded well with their own manhood. They haven't yet accepted the great, special fact of their own masculine identity.

Do you really *like a lot* your life as a man? Are you happy about being a guy? Have you aggressively grabbed hold of all that that means, its responsibilities and its privileges?

Your maleness is God's fabulous gift to you.

David prayed,

> You created my inmost being;
> You knit me together in my mother's womb (Ps. 139:13).

God made you correctly, and for strategic reasons and purposes; in your spot being a woman wouldn't do. Don't ever question your being a man.

> Who are you, O man, to talk back to God? Shall what is formed say to him who formed it, "Why did

11

you make me like this?" Does not the potter have the right to [make what he wants] (Rom. 9:20, 21)?

"Like clay in the hand of the potter, so are you in my hand," He declares (Jer. 18:6).

A man of faith includes in that faith the confidence that God knew what He was doing when He put him together—male equipment and all. He relaxes with that; he's secure.

You may be a Titus, Paul's disciple who loved to minister "with much enthusiasm and on his own initiative" (2 Cor. 8:17). You may be a Timothy, with tendencies to be insecure and hesitant (1 Cor. 16:10, 11; 2 Tim. 1:6–8). Both of them, full of faith and obedience, traveled and helped people everywhere.

You may be a Peter, rough and mouthy and conspicuous. Or a John, quiet and sensitive. Both of them wrote Holy Scripture and lived powerfully effective lives.

Are you a poet? A politician? Muscular? Intellectual? Huge? Small? Left brain? Right brain? However God created you, thank and worship Him for what He created! Wrote David,

> I praise you because I am fearfully and wonder-
>   fully made;
>   your works are wonderful,
>   I know that full well (Ps. 139:14).

Maybe your own flaw is serious. When God asked Moses to speak for Him and Moses objected that he wasn't eloquent, listen to God's response:

> Who gave man his mouth? Who makes him deaf
> or dumb? Who gives him sight or makes him blind? Is
> it not I, the Lord? Now go, and I will help you speak
> and will teach you what to say (Exod. 4:11, 12).

No whining, no alibis. Moses had a speaking problem; some scholars think he stuttered. But Moses decided to trust God and push out—and he became perhaps history's most powerful leader.

Maybe God is going to deliberately weaken you because of a specific, important purpose He has for you. Anne's back, legs, and feet are somewhat malformed—enough for God to force her off her feet and guide her to writing music and books.

Maybe God will weaken you *in spite of* His specific purpose for you. He made me mildly dyslexic—and then put me on the radio reading my messages five days a week! How do you figure that!

However He's made you, don't fight Him. Love His handiwork.

A "body beautiful" isn't necessarily a help. One of the guys I see at the health club is a physical Atlas, but his personal life is a mess. I say to him, "How's it going?" and he says, "Same ol', same ol' . . ." (Same old relational screw-ups, same old financial binds.)

Listen, God has given you "the gift of life" (1 Pet. 3:7). This is your very own life, the only earthly life you'll ever have.

> Always be thankful, for this is God's will for you
> who belong to Jesus Christ (1 Thess. 5:18, TLB).

But maybe you're saying, "Look, I'm not complaining over what God made when He made me; it's not God's fault, it's mine. I've ruined my life all by myself. I've got past sins that disqualify me; for me it's too late to go for the gold."

Hebrews says,

> See to it that no one misses the grace of God and
> that no bitter root grows up to cause trouble and de-
> file many (Heb. 12:15).

We men are to come together; we're to minister to each other; we're to love each other and help each other *make it*. The world— even the Christian world—is full of men who have debarred themselves from fullness of life in Christ. Why? They've missed God's grace.

What do you tell them? You're one beggar telling other beggars where to get bread. You tell them about God's "amazing grace"—that even "saved a wretch like me."

The great apostle Paul said he didn't deserve to be an apostle because for so many earlier years he'd persecuted Christians. "But by the grace of God I am what I am [he said], and His grace to me was not without effect" (1 Cor. 15:10).

You see, "all have sinned"! Even all *believers* have sinned. Everybody, *everybody's* at the same starting line. God's grace is equally available to each one. And His grace is great enough, powerful enough to reach deep into your soul and remove everything that would weaken you and disqualify you from finishing gloriously.

The same God who created you is strong enough to finish you with style! He's up to it! He's both "the Author *and Perfecter* of your faith" (Heb. 12:2).

Then don't allow memories of past sins to keep you a wimp. Believe God for His complete grace in your life. Hold up your head and, because of Him, start enjoying being *you.*

Beautiful black gospel singer Ethel Waters said it this way: "God don't sponsor no flops."

4 The myth of it's-not-what-you-do-it's-what-you-are

Ray again . . .

When I was a teenager I dreamed of being a cartoonist, or a newspaper man, or . . .

I knew God had called me to be a minister, but I was questioning the whole idea. I remember as a small boy, maybe seven, ramming around with my buddies in the basement of our church, when old Peter Englund stopped me, tousled my hair, and said, "Raymond, some day God's going to make you a preacher."

I was awed. Suddenly I knew he was right, and somehow, with his old hand upon my head, I felt ordained.

I grew up remembering that moment of God's call to me. In my college days, though, a seminary was adjacent to the football field where I tackled, passed, grunted and sweat with the rest of the team. There next door I could see all those future preachers—walking around with their mincing little steps and carrying their black briefcases. Ugh.

You remember what you dreamed about being when you were a kid, the career decisions you struggled with as you emerged into adulthood, and the thoughts you have now about whether you decided right or not . . .

Why is a guy's work such a big deal in his life? Because that's the way God first started him out. God made him, and then immediately He gave him a job to do:

> He formed Adam from the dust of the ground and breathed life into his nostrils. . . . And He took the man and put him in the Garden of Eden to work it and take care of it (Gen. 2:7, 15).

Anne and I had dinner the other night with our youngest, Nels, and his wife, Heather, and their two-month-old son, Bradford. God has helped Nels strongly establish a Christian home, but he's still struggling with the whole issue of career. Should he do this, or should he do that?

"Why do I care so much?" he asked. "Is that being self-centered?"

Oh, no. God cares a lot. He makes a man, and He guides him to the specific job He wants him to do. And God's going to show Nels. We pray a lot.

Don't feel guilty over taking your career seriously. That concern was built into you from the very beginning.

Work is part of God's plan for the whole world. He didn't create clothing; He only created wool and cotton. He didn't create bread and muffins, only grain. He didn't create metal, only ore. He lets people search and dig and discover and put together. And make and advertise and sell and buy. Through work. That's good.

Think about the Israelites during the forty years they didn't have to work; the whole time they produced no clothes, no housing, no food. They were fed daily allotments like animals in a zoo. And there never was a more cantankerous bunch of people!

We all need outflow, ministries, work to do to take our place, to help others, and to make the world go.

There's a reaction to this today, a backlash. Never mind what a man *does*, he needs to concentrate on what he *is*. Someone asks, "Aren't you Joe Smith, the football player?" He's supposed to answer, "No, I'm not a football player. I'm a man who plays football." And everybody's supposed to applaud his great sense of identity.

I think that's silly. He's a football player! He's also, hopefully, a Christian, and he may be a husband, a father, a good car mechanic, a harmonica player—a hundred things. And a piece of his identity is connected with each of those occupations and skills.

Poor guys! These days they really get picked on. If they give themselves to hard work their priorities are wrong, they're chasing after some illusion of self-worth, they're sacrificing their values for status . . .

Maybe. Or maybe they're just *working hard*—which 2 Thessalonians 3:6–13 says in the eyes of God is a very good thing.

Men in many occupations have affected their societies for God:

> David, a king;
> Amos, a rancher;
> Moses, a lawgiver;
> Joshua, a general;
> —and how about this?—Daniel, a man in the uneasy service of a despotic foreign government.

But whatever your job, God's working on you. He fills His world with bank tellers and well-diggers—most of all because He's maturing His people.

> With God our character is always paramount. That's why He set aside Moses when he was at his "John Wayne best" and sent him into the wilderness for forty years. It was to straighten out his character.
>
> It was well worth the time. God said later, "There is none like my servant Moses. . . ." [1]

It's never easy to be God's man at your work place—in "this world with devils filled." The philosophy of the world is completely upside-down from God's.

---

1. Gary Richmond, "In Pursuit of Manhood," *Psychology for Living,* June 1991, 7, 14.

The Bible says that success in your work is dependent on confidence in God. The world says that success is built on self-confidence and personal competence. And the world's philosophy can breed into any Christian—oh, so subtly—smugness and self-reliance. I appreciate what Robert Farrar Capon wrote:

> In heaven there are . . . no upright, successful types who, by dint of their own integrity, have been accepted into the great country club in the sky. There are only failures, only those who have accepted their deaths in their sins and who have been raised up by the King, Who Himself died that they might live.[2]

Moses warned the Israelites about the same thing, this temptation to feel elitist:

> When you have eaten and are satisfied, praise the Lord your God. . . . Be careful that you do not forget the Lord. . . . You may say to yourself, "My power and the strength of my hands have produced this wealth for me." But remember the Lord your God, for it is he who gives you the ability to produce wealth (Deut. 8:10, 11, 17, 18).

Work, then, comes from God, and He wants you to humbly receive it and enjoy it.

But what work? Which job? What does He want you to do? Well, forget bartending or running a strip joint . . . But of the millions of jobs which are basically guilt-free, which one is for you?

> The Lord will guide you always;
> he will satisfy your needs in a sun-scorched
> land [even in areas of economic depression];
> [He] will strengthen your frame (Isa. 58:11).

---

2. Quoted by Nathan Hatch in "The Perils of Being a Professional," *Christianity Today,* 11 Nov. 1991, 25.

Whether through circumstances or a wise Christian's counsel or a sermon or a verse of Scripture, God is committed to let you know His will. Be aggressive in seeking it, through prayer and the Word—and through training and job hunting . . .

But also, without anxiety,

> Wait for the Lord:
> be strong and take heart
> and wait for the Lord (Ps. 27:14).

When you know that what you're doing is God's will, at least for now, then in spite of difficulties and problems, you can love what you're doing. Love it because you know it's from His hand.

I have a card by the mirror where I shave that says, "Whatever you do, whether in word or in deed, do it all in the name of the Lord Jesus, giving thanks to God the Father through him" (Col. 3:17).

5 God at work in men at work

Anne writes . . .

Let me share with you some of the men Ray and I think are spiritual greats. The first one is from the Bible, and then four who are friends of ours follow: These are men who love God and love others—through their work.

Number One is so unknown in the Bible, we don't even have his name. He was one of Abraham's slaves, and he was a model for every man who has a job. (His story is found in Genesis, chapter 24.)

First, this fellow was conscientious in the way he obeyed authority. Abraham said, "Go back to the country I came from and find a wife for my son Isaac." (Obviously this man was trusted!)

His compliance was taken for granted; he only wanted to be sure he understood his boss's wishes: "If she refuses to come, what do I do then . . . ?"

Abraham said, "God will help you get the right one." He could talk to this godly servant in spiritual terms; he knew the man would understand.

Second, this was a fellow who practiced both general prayer ("O Lord, give me success") and specific prayer ("Lord, may the right girl be willing to give me a drink and water my camels, too")—all in the business of his work.

Third, he had the conditioned reflex-action of worship. When God answered his specific prayer and sent the right girl, the man "bowed down and worshiped the Lord." And when her family agreed to let her go, he worshiped God again.

Fourth, his tongue was ready to acknowledge God at work in his life—even to strangers. He'd never seen those people before, and yet before he was done with them I think they had a new confidence—confidence in a God who could so spectacularly answer prayer in an ordinary man's work life.

Or look at some modern examples.

Armin is a Lutheran minister, eighty years old and strong and fresh. Ray and I have known Armin and his wife, Reidun, for thirty years. Ray says he's never heard him grumble. He's always ready with the kind of a word that smiles. And before you leave Armin you bow together in prayer. He's that kind of guy. He loves God, he loves people, and he loves connecting the latter with the former.

We had dinner last night with Larry and Carol. Larry's an elementary school teacher. And Larry is Mister Enthusiasm; all the kids love him. He's also a volunteer assistant basketball coach at a local college, and he's helped direct numberless summer basketball camps for youngsters.

Larry just loves to help people, young or old. One time after Sunday church, he introduced Ray to a man who was 103 years old! Larry was high as a kite: "Pastor Ray, I just helped him come to know Jesus!"

John is our family doctor, pressed with overwork as are most good family doctors. But always when we see him two things shine through: his love for the Lord and his love of helping people.

"I feel as if I'm part of your ministry if I can help you stay well," he says to Ray and me. He looks into our eyes. He listens carefully. His schedule is tight—but he's not. And when something is of concern, he lays on kind hands and prays that God will heal.

Gordie fixes furnaces. Ray loves his brother Gordie. When Gordie was president of the governing board of our Lake Avenue Congregational Church, professional and financial big guns were happy to serve on the board under him. It was inevitable: Gordie was so outstanding and loved, there came a time when Ray asked him to come onto the pastoral staff of the church. We would have been honored.

But Gordie said, "Ray, I can't leave the gas company! I'm God's man there. He has called me to serve Him there, and I wouldn't trade places with anybody."

You can be sure all these men know problems. They get hassled in their work like anybody else. But they love God first! That makes their work of great importance—and shot through with prayer, with Spirit-directed integrity, with Christ-empowered wisdom, and with God-given perseverance.

6 An action plan for developing your life

Ray again . . .

A man only gets one whack at life. There are no reruns, no instant replays.

And you're playing hardball all the way, and the way the ump calls it, sticks. That's because the "ump" is God Himself.

The apostle Paul wrote, "So we make it our goal to please him" (2 Cor. 5:9). This was the same Paul who started poorly but finished well; that gives you hope! Then he wrote, "For we must all stand before the judgment seat of Christ, that each one may receive what is due him for the things done while in the body, whether good or bad" (2 Cor. 5:10).

Friend, each day you live is so important! You're going to have to answer for what you do, how you are. That's why even your reading this book, in this very time of your life, could be crucial.

Probably you do your work with the aid of schedules, appointments, plans, projections, budgets and goals. How about in your personal life—have you an action plan to get you where you want to go as a man of God, a whole person?

Let me share what's been my plan, my tool, much of my adult life: I live out of a notebook.[1] Nobody else's notebook is exactly like mine; you'd have to adapt yours to fit your own life.

The life goal I've chosen is Colossians 3:17:

> Whatever you do, whether in word or deed, do
> it all in the name of our Lord Jesus, giving thanks to
> God the Father through him.

In other words, my goal is to live for Christ and serve Him with a grateful heart. It's good to choose a life target of some sort, to shoot all your arrows toward the same mark.

My notebook is a tool to get all those parts of my life headed toward this goal. And I've got it organized so that it really is, you could say, my life between two covers.

I have eleven sections. Your notebook would be different, but let me describe mine, to give you the idea.

Section 1: Personal facts I need at my fingertips. Social security and passport numbers. Insurance policy information. Doctor's phone number. Important birthdays. Frequent-flyer numbers. List of those Christian workers Anne and I give to every month, and how much. Current financial balance sheet.

Section 2: My life purpose statement. The specific goals of this current year. A page of proverbs for men. I refer to this section often, to keep me focused.

Section 3: My current discipling group. A page for each man and a list of subjects we've covered in our meetings so far.

Section 4: Current personal Bible studies.

Section 5: Outline of my prayer concerns. This section is the guide to my regular quiet time. After I repeat daily affirmations, I pray through four divisions for prayer:

---

1. Anne and I put these together for anyone who wants to try the idea. Write us for a notebook brochure at 4500 Campus Drive, Suite 662, Newport Beach, California 92660.

A for adoration. Suggestions for worship. Three or four hymns to sing to Him.

C for confession. Areas I need to confess that I might not otherwise think of.

T for thanksgiving. Itemized blessings in my life.

S for supplication. One page each: my personal needs, Anne's needs, each of the children's. Personal finances. "Haven of Rest" radio needs, of which I'm speaker. Renewal Ministries needs, under which Anne and I speak at conferences. Our books and tapes. Our nation, its leaders. Missionaries, pastors, extended family, friends, unsaved.

This prayer section I consider crucial; if my prayer life gets messy, my life gets messy. The outline helps me get somewhere in my prayers; I sense I make progress here in my relationship with the Lord.

Section 6: Personal journaling. I'm accountable to my small group of guys to journal three days a week.

Section 7: Information and future ideas for Renewal Ministries.

Section 8: "Haven of Rest" broadcast information. Program information. Broadcast dates. Messages. Current finances.

Section 9: Daily calendar pages. To-do's. Appointments. I also do a week-at-a-glance page each Monday.

Section 10: Monthly planning calendars, strategic for planning our conference speaking.

Section 11: Alphabetized tabbed pages for addresses and phone numbers.

The front and back pockets hold calling cards, credit cards, a family picture, a scratch pad . . .

Whenever I go, my notebook goes. I live out of it. It keeps me organized, focused, making progress.

You could do the same—and get all those bits of paper out of your pockets and all those little notebooks into one comprehensive one. Always present. Always ready to serve you.

Keep your life in front of you—in a notebook. Are you loving God? Are you loving others? Are you keeping the parts of your life analyzed, pared or expanded, up to date, prayed over?

On the other hand, if you ever lose your notebook . . . have mercy.

PART II

Your Love for God

7 Business no, romance yes

Ray writes . . .

I was saying, we men need a great, Spirit-empowered move back to love—love for God and love for others.

Let's start with your love for God. The way a man thinks of his own life depends on the way he thinks of God.

Many men consider God above them—awesome, unattainable—so they keep their distance. Even the church guys with this God-view stand around on the church steps after the service and don't get too involved with the hard-core "religious" types.

Other men think God is below them—effeminate, boring, too germ-free, too "nice." Probably their Sunday school teachers were all women, and their impression of Jesus is that He had sad eyes and brown curls. These fellows keep their distance, too. If they're still going to church, they hang out on the edges of things with the "real guys" who can yuck over dirty jokes out of the sides of their mouths. The ones who don't get too judgmental about messing around.

Possibly, even if you deny it, you think of God as your equal, your rival.

31

(When God first created man and made him ruler of the earth, He knew well that He was creating a potential rival. Actually, that ought to make real guys take a second look at God, thinking, "I admire that; I like riskers.")

But if God is ostensibly your rival, you're another Jacob; you wrestle Him. Maybe, if the truth were known, God vaguely bugs you. You're a *man*. You want to stand tall, strong and complete in yourself—self-governed, self-reliant, self-defined, self-contained—an authentic model of the "self-made man."

You have the uneasy feeling that God threatens that image. When occasionally—by mistake?—you catch His eye, you really do know what He wants. You know He's waiting for you to surrender that male ego and yield to Him completely.

"Love God," as this part title says? Maybe you want to love Him just a *little*—just enough to get to heaven.

One time Anne and I sat at lunch discussing speaking dates and book writing until I'd had enough.

I leaned across the table. "Anne," I said, "I want you to keep in mind one thing: what we have between us isn't a business partnership, it's a romance."

God, hopefully even through these pages, is leaning across your table. (You see, a love thing with God always starts with His initiative.)

He says to you, "I want you to understand something. My purpose in designing and making you in the first place, and My purpose in sending My Son Jesus Christ wasn't only to save you from hell—although that's included. It was so that we could be best friends and love each other. This isn't a business deal, it's a romance."

Maybe you've been noticing a certain associate at work and you think, "I like him. I wish we could get beyond the business level. I wish sometime he'd contact me, not about work but just to get together."

That's how God feels about you.

If you're the typical Christian male your contacts with Him are all business: "Lord, help me today, . . . bless me, . . . be with So-and-so, . . . protect me . . ."

God is looking for a lot more than that. (A Pharisee named Simon once had Jesus to dinner; that seems like a commendable thing to do. But Jesus said, "Simon, you didn't give me a kiss. . . .")

"Business partners" are okay, of course; they help make your life hang together. But they're just shopping lists; they're to-do's. A real love for God begins to develop when you contact Him for Himself: "I love You, Lord . . ."

Do it now, while you're reading . . .

In fact, "business partners" alone are actually dangerous—you think you've done your spiritual duty and that's it. Old Puritan Richard Alleine wrote, "Let not prayers or hearing sermons be instead of a God to thee!"

Would I be content with forever sitting across a lunch table with Anne discussing speaking dates?

No—

No way—

No how.

Hey, I'm looking for sex, I'm looking for loyalty, I'm looking for deep happiness together. I'm looking for common plans and shared jokes and dark evenings alone. I'm looking for the look across a crowded room that says, "I'm yours." I'm looking for security, for intimacy, for a best friend.

Every guy's a romantic, an idealist. He's got dreams. And God is saying to us men, "Look, I give the gift of marriage, but it's only a reflection of the real thing. I Myself want a love relationship with you that's ultimate.

"If you're willing to really learn to love Me, I promise you these things and many more: the assurance that your sins are forever wiped clean, personal joy that explodes into motivation and strength, courage to achieve and conquer, perspective and wisdom for the darkest times, and the feel of a grip of love that never lets you go.

"How do I give you these things? I give them as you learn to love Me with all your heart, soul, strength, and mind. They're the bonus-checks, the love-gifts, I return to you."

What kind of love does God have for you? Well, He describes it in many places in the Bible—like Ezekiel 16, the book of Hosea, and Ephesians 5—and if you're a believer, you see that what He's got for you is a conjugal relationship.

And your strongest passion as a man must be a reciprocal marital chastity toward God.

That poor guy at the athletic club who puts cars and boats at the top of his love-list is adulterous. Any hankering after status and stuff more than God is a gross act of infidelity.

And Satan thinks up plenty more rival loves: adulterous women (Prov. 5:3–23; 7:4–27), homosexual men (Rom. 1:18–27; 1 Cor. 6:9, 10), work and career (Ps. 127:2; Prov. 23:4, 5; Isa. 55:2), leisure and play (James 5:1–6), and simply all the subtle and treacherous ramifications of Self (Rom. 2:8; 2 Tim. 3:1–2).

How would you feel if you discovered your wife was cheating on you? That's how God feels if you're playing around on Him. How would you feel about your wife's lovers? That's how God feels about your "idols." No wonder idolatry is mentioned more often than any other problem in the Bible! God's emotions are ripped and torn up by a man's substitute-loves.

"Dear children," says First John's punch line, "keep yourselves from idols." In that case . . .

> The dearest idol I have known,
>   Whate'er that idol be,
> Help me to tear it from Thy throne
>   And worship only Thee![1]

The Ephesian Christians publicly burned all their idols—at a cost of almost half a year's typical salary (Acts 19:19). Paul said the power of the early Christians was that they "turned *to God from idols"* (1 Thess. 1:9). Nobody can hang onto both, any more than your wife could be thrilled and satisfied with you while she's preoccupied with other men.

Listen: *any man, married or single, must first of all, most of all, in his heart be monogamous to God.*

---

1. From "O for a Closer Walk with God," William Cowper, 1772.

He says to you,

> Place me like a seal over your heart,
>> like a seal over your arm;
> for love is as strong as death,
>> its jealousy unyielding as the grave.
> It burns like blazing fire,
>> like a mighty flame.
> Many waters cannot quench love;
>> rivers cannot wash it away.
> If one were to give
>> all the wealth of his house for love,
>> it would be utterly scorned (Song of Sol. 8:6–7).

8 Spiritually "sleeping around"

<u>Ray again</u> . . .

One way or another, God made us men love to love! If we don't love God, then, with all our heart, soul, strength, and mind, we'll spend that love on something/someone else. In other words, we'll sleep around.

Why should we do that? Why would even a Christian guy do that? For the same reason married women can be unfaithful: if they love themselves more than they love their husbands. Then their mind-set is, "I like the perks of being his wife, but I want to be free to make my own sexual choices." The trouble is, until she's willing to bend her ego, her Self, toward her husband, and surrender her heart to him alone, their marriage is nothing.

Many a guy says, by inference, "I'm glad to be known as a Christian, but I want to make my own decisions. I'll go to church, I'll even do church work, but don't get any closer than that. . . ."

This fellow keeps jockeying for position to keep his Self intact and unbowed. "Entertain me—make me laugh, make me

cry—but don't make me give too much of myself." And he surren-
ders himself instead to his little opinions and activities and familiar
pleasures and habits.

In other words, he sleeps around.

Ego, pride, Self—that rival of God which is the ultimate
idol—stiff-arms not only God but love and joy and everything
great. "Love comes from God" (1 John 4:9).

Or change the metaphor. A man who prioritizes himself
above God is a cut plant. He's withered, drying, dying. He may
be the big joker who knows everybody and has a thousand ready
comments on news, weather, and sports; or he may be a loser—
withdrawn, insecure, isolated. In either case he's not well attached
to the Source.

What happens to him? His manhood doesn't develop. He
shrivels into a wimp. He has little or no courage against sexual
lusts, greed for money, jealousy, intemperance, arrogance. God's
law says "Thou shalt not"—but he says, "I'm sorry but I'm only
human. Gimme a break."

No guts, no glory.

What happens to a man who loves God? In times of temptation he hears God's love say to him, "I won't let you." And the man
believes that and stands tall.

The law condemns us because we break it. God's love builds
strength into us so that we *won't* break it.

One particular March, a successful engineer in our small
group confessed to us a major struggle in his heart. He'd had several extra projects that year apart from his company that had paid
really big bucks. He was wrestling with how much of his extra
earnings to divulge to the government in his income tax report.
In fact, he said he'd overspent, and if he told all, there was no
way he could pay what he owed.

Here was a guy we all really loved, and that night we bore
his burden with him. We prayed fervently that God would em-
power him with the courage to tell the truth. Even so, in our hearts
we knew what he would do.

The apostle Paul had said long ago, "The love of Christ constrains me." And the love of Christ constrained—pushed, pressed—our buddy on April 15. He spelled out his full income, he borrowed, he paid his whole tax bill.

And he grew. He grew to ten feet tall in our eyes that spring; he stood tall in the courageous integrity of a true man of God.

> He who walks righteously
> > and speaks what is right,
> who rejects gain from extortion
> > and keeps his hand from accepting bribes,
> who stops his ears against plots of murder
> > and shuts his eyes against contemplating evil—
> this is the man who will dwell in the heights,
> > whose refuge will be the mountain fortress.
> His bread will be supplied,
> > and water will not fail him (Isa. 33:15–16).

A man's love-relationship with God makes the difference.

Joseph, "well built and handsome" (Gen. 39:6), refused the sexual advances of his boss's wife because of the precedence of his love for God. "How could I do such a wicked thing and sin against God?" he said (Gen. 39:6).

The God-given hunger in every man's gut is to stand tall and be strong and complete. His love for God—and only his love for God—accomplishes that: It "keeps him from falling" (Jude 24), and makes him stand "strong in the Lord and in his mighty power" (Eph. 6:10–13).

9 Six ways for a man to love God

<u>Ray again</u> . . .

It was an expert in the law—a lawyer or maybe a legislator or a judge—to whom Jesus said, "Love the Lord your God with all your heart and with all your soul and with all your mind and with all your strength" (Mark 12:30). Even law experts aren't exempt from needing this advice. Our former neighbor was a sharp lawyer; now he's in prison.

How do you love God?

First, you establish the relationship. You come to Him acknowledging your sins and receiving His Son Jesus Christ to be the Savior who paid the penalty for everything in you that offends God.

> Christ died for our sins according to the Scriptures, he was buried, he rose again on the third day (1 Cor. 15:3–4).
>
> Repent, then, and turn to God, so that your sins may be wiped out (Acts 3:19).

This is the great hinge that opens the door.

You'll never stand tall as a man unless first you bow.

You'll never be a success unless first you admit that without Him you're a failure.

You'll never be a good man unless first you confess that in yourself you're bad.

That's number one. Right now, my friend, make that deal with Him, in your heart. Exchange your sins for His perfect right–eousness, your weakness for His power!

Then comes the outside job, which proves that the inside job was real. Even a current secular author says a man needs to commit himself first to that higher priority: "A father, in order to do that, may have to resist his own insistence that his life belongs to his work, his children, and his marriage."[1]

Exactly! It can't—although, if he resists this insistence, his work, his children, and his marriage will ultimately benefit wonderfully. But, as Vernard Eller says, "The person who takes his commitment to Christ seriously must travel light, giving up some involvements in order to make other involvements more truly revolutionary."[2]

You turn from idols to God. Anne says you "eliminate and concentrate." If you commit yourself to love Him, you'll order your whole life to that commitment. And you'll get integrated, you'll get satisfied, you'll grow up.

Let me suggest six ways to develop your love for God.

Now, suddenly this is going to get nitty-gritty. It has to! Any great love-relationship is built on little hour-by-hour decisions.

1. Worship Him, publicly and privately. There's no one else in the universe you're to worship; hopefully you love your wife, but don't worship her.

---

1. Robert Bly, *Iron John* (Redding, MA: Addison-Wesley, 1990), 134.
2. *The Simple Life* (Grand Rapids, MI: Eerdmans, 1973) 27.

But God is looking for those who will "worship him in spirit and in truth" (John 4:23, 24). In your regular church-going and in the rest of your life, adore Him, and tell Him so often. You start to bond with your wife when you tell her over and over what you love about her; you start to bond with God the same way.

To get the hang of it, sit before Psalms 145–150, and talk to Him about what you read there. The Bible is full of worship sections which can model for you a style of how to tell Him what you think of Him.

2. Give sacrificially of your money. That's drastic, but sincere love for God is drastic, it's revolutionary. Jesus said, "Do not store up for yourselves treasures on earth . . . but store up for yourselves treasures in heaven. . . . No one can serve two masters. Either he will hate the one and love the other, or he will be devoted to the one and despise the other. You cannot serve both God and money" (Matt. 6:19–20, 24).

He says, "Don't store up on earth *for yourselves*, but store up in heaven *for yourselves*"; did you catch that? Either way, you do it for yourself. But He says what you store up for yourself on earth you're going to lose, but what you give to Him, you're actually stashing away for your own future in heaven.

Sometimes a guy puts money into the offering plate at church, and he pictures that bill with wings on it! And he thinks, "Well, I'll never see that money again." Wrong. That's the only money he ever *will* see again. He's simply transferring his funds. Interesting: you have it in your power, by loving God with your money, to make yourself rich in heaven.

God tests your love for Him to see how literally you'll believe Him. "Give, and it will be given to you," He tells you (Luke 6:38). "Live by faith, not by sight" (2 Cor. 5:7). When you do that you start to learn to walk by inner directions, and you get strong.

How much should you give? If a tithe is new to you, begin with that; that's ten percent of your salary. God says you're *robbing* Him if you give Him less than that (Mal. 3:7–10). But live on ninety? Hey, some people have found out that God blessed them so much, they eventually gave Him ninety and lived on ten.

Because I've usually had jobs where I got regular pay checks, I've written the check for my tithe to Him the first of all my bills. It's been a symbol to me that I want to love Him first and most.

The point is that meaningful, regular giving will release Self's grip on you and give you a heart of ease, generosity, and joy.

Psalm 112 describes the godly man; read what he's like and copy him. For instance,

> Good will come to him who is generous and lends
>   freely,
> His heart is steadfast, trusting in the Lord. . . .
> He has scattered abroad his gifts to the poor,
>   his righteousness endures forever;
>   his [dignity] will be lifted high in honor
>   (Ps. 112:5, 7, 9).

3. Read the Bible daily. Anne and I separately read through the Bible every year. About five pages a day and you'll make it.[3] The flow, the connections, the development of meanings, and above all, the wisdom, is wonderful; it's helped us love God more and understand Him better, to read the whole of His love-letter to us, over and over. If this is new to you, start with *The Living Bible.* Otherwise, you might consider *The New International Version.*

4. Memorize the Bible. As a young man I joined the navy and got discipled by an older Christian who was merciless: "How many Bible verses have you memorized? Only about ten? Where have you been all your life? How many guys have you witnessed to lately? Maybe one? Don't you have any guts?"

Meeting this man was almost the best thing that ever happened to me. I took my love for God seriously and got busy. You can get the same Navigator cards that I got—Scripture verses you tuck into your pocket or over your car visor to help you start

---

3. Or subscribe, as we do, to *The Daily Walk,* P.O. Box 478, Mount Morris, IL 61054, phone 1-800-877-5539.

4. The Navigators, P.O. Box 6000, Colorado Springs, CO 80934.

living and breathing the Word of God.[4] When you're away from your Bible His words will still be "a lamp to your feet and a light to your path" (Ps. 119:105).

5. Mediate on the Bible. Chew it over, think about it, digest it. "Do not let this book of the Law depart from your mouth; meditate on it day and night, so that you may be careful to do everything written in it. Then you will be prosperous and successful" (Josh. 1:8).

Let these truths become the warp and woof of you, so that you think as He thinks, and you share His values and priorities.

6. Pray. How? Talk to Him inside yourself through the day. As often as you remember Him, keep a running conversation going. "Pray continually," says 1 Thessalonians 5:17. My personal tendency is to forget, so I stick notes on my shaving mirror, visor, desk, that say "PTP" ("Practice the Presence"), to gang up on myself.

But the fact is, you can't really develop intimacy with God on the run, squeezing it in between everything else. It involves changes, cuts, sacrifices.

Listen to James 4:8: "Come near to God and he will come near to you. Wash your hands, you sinners, and purify your hearts, you double-minded."

It's our constant need. These years of my life God has given me two companies to run, with offices sixty miles apart, plus a lot of air traveling. But everybody eats breakfast, right? So most mornings I eat alone in a restaurant where I'm not known, and there I meet God and read my Bible and write out my prayers. I'm no spiritual giant, but it's where He gets my heart happy and connected to Him.

David wrote his prayers; that's what the Psalms are!

George Washington wrote his prayers. Here is one, written on the battlefield:

> Direct my thoughts, words and work, wash away my sins in the immaculate blood of the Lamb, and purge my heart by the Holy Spirit. . . .
>
> Daily frame me more and more into the likeness of Thy Son Jesus Christ. . . .

Someone I can't identify wrote these words:

> A man is never so tall as when he kneels before
> God. Never more dependable than when he depends
> upon God. Never so strong as when he draws upon
> God's strength. Never so wise as when, in his lack of
> wisdom, he seeks divine guidance. Truly, the man who
> relies on God the most will be the most reliable man.

It's been the habit of the "greats." David, that mighty king, frequently "sat before the Lord" (2 Sam. 7:18). Daniel, that magnificent prophet, "three times a day got down on his knees and prayed, giving thanks to his God" (Dan. 6:10).

> Decide on your place, and be there.
> Decide on your time, and keep it.
> Be regular, be faithful, and remember—get
> 'way beyond those "business prayers."

Anne and I spoke at a conference recently for a church in Holland, where an American oil company executive said in front of the whole congregation, "Hold me accountable; I want to get to my office an hour early every morning and lock my door and spend that time with God. Ask me if I'm doing this; pester me about it!" This fellow knew it was his greatest need. He knew that strengthening his love for God would strengthen and purify all the other parts of his life.

God longs for you to move in close. And it's what you've been looking for all your life—and maybe didn't know it.

10 How God plugged a hole in my heart

Ray again . . .

Malcolm Forbes, Dr. Robert E. Gould, Dr. Martin Guggenheim, and several other "heavies" participated in a panel for *Vogue Magazine* on "American Men: What Do They Want?"

They concluded that American men want what men everywhere want:

> Men want love. Men want intimacy. The problem is they don't know how to achieve this and how to express it. From the earliest day on, boys are taught to be macho—not to show emotions, not to cry, not to show weakness. This means that we cannot share with another person equally and openly. If you cannot do that, you cannot love.[1]

Dr. Gould, speaking here, is actually echoing Proverbs 19:22: "What a man desires is unfailing love."

---

1. *Vogue,* June 1986, 237–38.

God is the Source, friend, of all the love you've been looking for—and which can never be found in a wife, mother, child, or best friend. When you yield to Him, your dammed-up Self is at last broken open, and you're finally ready to let in all the vast flow of the real thing.

I was a boy who grew up with a hole in my heart. My dad was a fine Christian man, but five days a week he was a traveling salesman, which meant he was mostly an absentee father. Beyond that, I was the last child of five, born into a house not large enough to hold that fifth baby. (Does that tell you I was a surprise?)

It was a wonderful family; it just seemed complete without me. My two older brothers, who were my heroes, did everything together. Then came two older sisters, who were best friends. Then there was little Ray.

When each day ended somebody would say, "It's bedtime, Ray. Go on to bed," and I'd leave the house and go sleep at my aunt's, next door. I wondered, was I basically an extra? Was I just the brat, or were they really glad they had me? (They were, but I didn't know it.)

So I grew up unsure of myself—full of dreams to be somebody and do something, but full of fears I wouldn't make it. I was a determined Christian, but I had a hole in my heart.

Then God gave me a friend. Her name was Anne, and on our honeymoon, for the first time ever, I poured out to her my hurts and my doubts about myself.

But Anne believed in me. At last I had a friend who, from the first until now, has loved me and encouraged me and affirmed me. Every man needs a friend like that.

I grew—and I began to see that all that encouragement didn't come primarily from Anne. If it had, I might have spent my life running after her and sucking more juices out of her than she had to give.

I began to learn that it was God who, most of all, loved me and wanted to encourage me—and that He chose to do it partially through Anne. And she just took her orders from God, as I sought to.

I learned that real love—which builds men who are manly and courageous to dream, dare, do, attack, conquer—doesn't come *from* any other human but only, at the most, *through*.

All along, you see, there stands God in your life. He made you, He knows you, He loves you thoroughly. And He says, "Look, parts of My love—bits and pieces of it—come to you through humans: parents or wife or children or friends . . .

"But turn to Me, Myself! Draw fully from Me; I am everything you long for. I am all that your male psyche has been incomplete without. I am your true Father. I am your true Lover. I Myself am love!"

I'm starting to grow up.

And not only has the hole in my heart healed over, the scar tissue makes it stronger than it would have been otherwise.

11 "The Lord is close" (Ps. 34:18)

Anne writes . . .

Our daughter Sherry gave birth to her son Drew by C-section. Then unwashed Drew was simply handed over to his dad, Walt, and temporarily forgotten—while Sherry, full of problems, got the medical team's undivided attention. So for the first half hour of Drew's life his dad was bending over him, singing to him, cuddling him, whispering to him, rocking him, petting him.

There's been a special connection between those two ever since. Who was the most affected by those thirty minutes? Undoubtedly, Walt. When Drew forgets the bond, Walt doesn't. When Drew is temporarily rebellious or thoughtless, Walt yearns over him as strongly as ever. Drew drifts off; Walt remains constant.

But Drew, I suspect, will have a lifelong impression, buried back in his subconscious, that his dad Walt loves him and is there above him somewhere, very close.

They say that the few inches in front of your face is the most intimate part of you, the space last to be violated. ("You're in my face," people say, or "Get out of my face.")

What do you think: Did Adam live all his life with a faint memory of his first conscious moments, when God was breathing into his nose—when God was in his face?

God's memory of that primeval experience is more vivid than man's, of course. He remembers perfectly that when He made him He loved him, His Spirit brooded over him, He bent down and breathed into him; maybe He cuddled him and crooned to him. Zephaniah 3:17 talks about God's taking great delight in His creation, quieting him with love, and rejoicing over him with singing.

Through his life a guy may forget that bond; God doesn't. Through all his straying (so many men in prison, so few in church!), God still remembers how he started . . . and God yearns for that closeness again.

Remember Jesus' story about the prodigal son? Luke talks about the boy's rebellious desertion, crashing failure on his own, and decision to go back home, even if in a lesser capacity.

> But when he was still a long way off, his father [an obvious picture of God] saw him and was filled with compassion for him; he ran to his son, threw his arms around him and kissed him (Luke 15:20).

I understand that the original Greek word "kissed" implies continuous action: He went on kissing him and kissing him! Maybe God was remembering His closeness with Adam, and longing for that again . . .

Or look at the Father-God's words to Israel in Hosea:

> I was the one who taught Israel to walk. I took my people up in my arms, but they did not acknowledge that I took care of them. I drew them to me with affection and love. I picked them up and held them to my cheek. . . .
>
> How can I give you up, Israel? My love for you is too strong (Hos. 1:3–4, TEV).

And what about your average guy? Maybe there's a lifelong impression, a faint memory buried deep in his subconscious, that in his long-ago beginnings God was "in his face" . . . and that He still loves him and hovers over him, . . . that He's close, longing for the man to turn and respond.

The potential to be best friends with God is nearer than the average male realizes. If I were a mystic, I'd say like maybe an inch or so away.

PART III

Your Love for Your Wife

12 The bane/blessing of a wife

Ray writes . . .

Aleksandr Solzhenitsyn, the Russian writer, says, "Men have forgotten God; that's why all this has happened."

He's right. First we love God. Then we love others.

But our deep love for God—or lack of it—determines how we love others; in fact, it determines everything about us.

When we forget God, craziness breaks out. And all those resulting external pressures collapse us men into peculiar shapes— maybe into playboys, or cowboys, or most recently assistant women.

The playboy-type doesn't have any feelings. He's the James Bond kind with the cold, steely eyes, who treats women as consumer commodities.

The cowboy has feelings, but they're locked up inside. He's the John Wayne, strong-silent type who's courteous but awkward around women. So after he's done his duty by her, he has his horse (or car) parked right outside so he can ride off immediately to whatever his highly important business is.

Men who become assistant women do for their wives what they probably never did for their mothers: chores. Certainly God's kind of leadership includes lots of concern and tenderness and servanthood—but that's different from a man's becoming feminized. If he is, then the children have a mother and an assistant mother, and they still have no real father at all.

But playboys, cowboys, and assistant women all live with an inner anxiety. Somehow they know they're not becoming well-rounded; they're not growing up to stand tall and strong in their homes and in society as God's men. They don't love God first and most, so they have no idea how to relate to others.

You want to love God, with all your heart, soul, strength, and mind.

And you want to love others as yourself. *Especially your wife.*

Anne and I were out the other night to dinner with friends. Marty was complaining that Brad could have more "dates" with her and their grown daughter, but he won't. "They just talk woman-talk," he growled.

It heightened our suspicion that Dr. Daniel Levinson is right—he says he doesn't think that men like women very well.[1] Well, little boys don't normally like girls, and girls aren't supposed to like boys. So they grow up quite separate and unfamiliar with each other. Consequently, normally, grown-up women have zero men friends, and men have zero women friends. And they have no idea how to reach across the great chasm—except sexually, which is another thing altogether.

So when they marry, they're like a couple of porcupines in Alaska. Whenever they pull apart from each other they get cold. So to get warm they draw together, but then they needle each other. So they spend their whole lives either feeling cold or needling each other.

God didn't start out marriage to be that way. *Think about the excitement when it first began:*

---

1. *The Seasons of a Man's Life* (New York: Ballentine Books, 1978), 121.

Adam takes his first look at this wonderful creation, Eve, and he exclaims,

"**This is now** . . ."

(I've finally got the beat! This is the music and the rhythm of my life that I've been waiting for!)

". . . **bone of my bones** . . ."

(Look, she's got my structure, and I've got her structure!)

". . . **and flesh of my flesh**. . . ."

(She's different from the other creations. My kind of life is her kind of life; I can finally define myself— in terms of her).[2]

Understand, as if it were the first time ever, what you've got when you've got a wife. You have a personal counterpart, an echo of yourself who's like you but different, designed by God just to fit to you.

Adam had looked at horses, dragonflies, pigeons and guppies, but never before had he seen a counterpart to himself.

Recently our much-loved adopted son Nels had his own first child. Anne and I were there in the hospital in the middle of the night when that little boy made his appearance, and after a bit Nels came out to be with us. Together we three peered through the glass, and Nels exclaimed, "There's my own flesh and blood!" And we realized that in all his almost-twenty-nine years of living, Nels had never before seen with his own eyes another person who was his own flesh and blood! Nels knows well how much his family loves him, but tiny Bradford Nelson Ortlund is different and special.

Now, look at your wife, not as a porcupine in Alaska but through God's eyes. That's the realistic look, the *right* look. You find it in His Book.

God says, *enjoy her body*. It's not only hers, it's yours (1 Cor. 7:14). "May her breasts satisfy you always" (Prov. 5:19); may she

---

2. Thoughts borrowed from Rousas John Rushdoon, writing in *The Counsel of Chalcedon Magazine*, 22.

become in your eyes, when she comes to you, "like one bringing contentment" (Song of Sol. 8:10).

God says, *enjoy her insights.* Think about what God told Abraham: "Listen to whatever Sarah your wife tells you" (Gen. 21:12).

God says, *enjoy her accomplishments.* The husband in Proverbs praises his wife, saying, "Many women do noble things, but you surpass them all" (Prov. 31:28–29).

God says, *enjoy her status before Him.* He says she's an "heir with you of the gracious gift of life" (1 Pet. 3:7).

God says *enjoy*—not selfishly but humbly and gratefully—*what she adds to your life.* God made woman to be a "helper suitable" for you (Gen. 2:18). She's His gift to you, *created for you* (1 Cor. 11:9).

Further, generally speaking, God says "Two are better than one, because they have a good return for their work" (Eccles. 4:9). Your gifts and your woman's gifts can probably fit together better than you've yet explored and discovered.

Anne often skim-reads for me, with me, when I'm preparing sermons. Together we teach most conference material side by side, conversationally. She edits my radio scripts and sometimes important letters. She finishes my stuff and makes it sound more like me than me!

On the other hand, having me, Anne gets a better return for her work, as well: what she learns from my preaching and teaching often goes into her books and speaking . . . Besides, I'm good for hanging pictures and cleaning the fishpool and carrying out the trash.

But hey—it's not first a business partnership, it's a romance. The last thing we do in bed every night, wrapped in each other's arms, is pray for one another. Alone in elevators sometimes we kiss passionately, one pinning the other against a wall so we'll get caught when the doors open. In airports, sometimes we separate so we can pretend to find each other accidentally: "Anne Ortlund! What are you doing in Dallas/Minneapolis/Tokyo?" That's good for extra hugs and kisses.

We've found that tested and proved love brings great delight (Song of Sol. 1:2).

There are thousands of books on the testing and proving. Our plan isn't to drag you through all the adjustments and mutually inflicted sufferings and losses that have brought us to this point of delight. Each couple's agonies are uniquely their own, and those agonies must be hacked and fought through to the other side. Our Model Jesus, "for the joy set before him, endured the cross" (Heb. 12:2).

All we want to do here—in this age of victimization and recovery and codependence and boundaries and space and entitlements—is to warn you against the bogs you can get stuck in so you never reach the other side at all.

When the two of you clash—and you will, because everybody does—don't start over-inspecting yourself and don't start over-inspecting the other; don't begin with human-oriented solutions.

Charles Krauthammer's recent commencement address at McGill University included these words:

> You have been rightly taught Socrates' dictum that the unexamined life is not worth living. I would add: The too examined life is not worth living either.
>
> Perhaps previous ages suffered from a lack of self-examination. The Age of Oprah does not. One of the defining features of modernity is self-consciousness. . . .
>
> The reigning cliché of the day is that in order to love others one must first learn to love oneself. The formulation—love thyself, then thy neighbor—is a license for unremitting self-indulgence, because the quest for self-love is endless. . . .
>
> Yes, examine. But do it with dispatch and modesty and then get on with it: Act and go and seek and do.[3]

---

3. "Beware the Study of Turtles," *Time* essay, 28 June 1993, 76.

When you do clash, go easy on all the fads *du jour.* The current ones are critical reviewings of your respective psyches, probings into your pasts, testings of your techniques of communication, et cetera, et cetera ad nauseam.

When you clash, look to Jesus! Better still, *before* you clash, look to Him. Make it your consistent discipline to read the Bible together and to pray, so that when clashes come, so do His solutions. "Husbands," says Ephesians 5:25–27, "make her holy [by] cleansing her by the washing with water through the word."

It's your responsibility, husband, to wash her—although you probably need it as much as she does.

13 Exploring your woman

Ray again . . .

When Anne and I have any distance to go in the car, she drives. That's because I can read in the car and she can't; she gets carsick. Once we'd spent a day in the desert studying Romans for my upcoming preaching—only we had a difference of opinion over a certain interpretation. The more we debated it, the more heated we got; the more heated we got, the heavier Anne's foot got on the accelerator.

We got a ticket.

End of debate.

A while back I wrote this about Christian marriage for a radio broadcast script:

> Christian friendship in marriage is built on thinking about life together—believing in Christ together. It's more than deciding what to do about the leaky faucet or when to plant the tulip bulbs. A couple who communicates mostly on that level is in trouble. They're just

living together. That's not what we're talking about.
[Business no, romance yes!]

Close friendship opens up and talks. It digs deep
into each other's beliefs and feelings and opinions and
blind spots and pleasures and hurts.[1]

Ray, Jr., was commenting on this the other day. He said one
of the surprises in being a husband is discovering what he hadn't
known before about Jani—or maybe even what he thought he
knew, which was completely off.

Ray said, "It's amazing and wonderful. I'm discovering all the
time that being a husband is being an explorer."

I see in front of me, on a scrap of paper, my funny Anne has
scribbled this:

Get deeply, deeply into the insides of your wife.
Can you imagine a pianist playing Rachmaninoff stand-
ing up?

Rachmaninoff is Russian soul-music; you have to dig to the
bottoms of the keys to make those tones powerful and sonorous.

Husbands, remember—business no, romance yes! To talk
business with your wife, all you need is computer-touch fingers.
But for a long-lived love affair—to bring out the music in her—
get down. Ask questions. Be respectful but searching. First Peter
3:7 (KJV) says "live with her according to knowledge." And the
longer you love her and know her, the more deeply you can
handle her.

Total openness takes both time and courage. When on our
honeymoon I poured out to Anne my doubts about myself, it was
painful—but more important than I could know. We took another
big step toward becoming real friends. And these days we're rich
to have several people—couples and singles—with whom "we
share our mutual woes, our mutual burdens bear."

---

1. "Haven of Rest" radio script, 18 November 1991.

Several months ago as we were in the car I opened my heart to Anne about a current fear. She began to "preach" at me concerning what I was struggling with, and I had to say, "Anne, I wasn't asking for your advice; I just wanted your listening ear. I just wanted to tell you how I'm feeling." She got the point.

A few weeks later we were in the car again, and Anne began to pour out to me a problem she was wrestling with. I offered her a few tons of Scripture verses and some magnificent thoughts, and she said, "Ray, I didn't tell you this for your advice; I just needed your listening ear. I wanted to tell you how I'm feeling." Oh, okay.

We're still learning, still stumbling sometimes, but the general tone of our relationship is delight. We have trouble keeping our hands off each other. The loving words keep spilling out. We're nuts about each other.

Her car license plate says "RAY ANNE."

Mine says "ANNE RAY."

I tell you, all a man's got is a pathetic substitute when a man's best friend is his dog.

14 A word from the rib

Anne writes . . .

If a man may have a dim, primeval memory of God's closeness above him, breathing into his nostrils as he first came to consciousness—does a woman have some faint memory of being lifted out of his side?

Maybe so. I personally love Ray's side; I feel comfortable there. When I'm pressed against his side or lying on his chest I have a sense of feeling at home, where I most belong. That part of him is most truly Ray; it's the cage that houses his heart, his lungs, his vital organs, his very life.

I have that same pleasure when I walk in step with him, feeling his side against me. I would say, of all places, that's where I most like to be: close to his side. I've never asked another wife if she feels this way.

I would think that any woman, married or not, likes to feel "side by side" with men. Maybe that's why the struggle to come from below him is so justified, and why the struggle to rise above him is so unnatural.

How can a man please this wife of his? By bringing her to his side. One of my greatest satisfactions is speaking at conferences with Ray, side by side, conversationally back and forth, which is the style that he's designed for us. People tell us it teaches volumes about marriage without our ever mentioning the word . . . This book is another example. He loves to include me in his life when it works, and I affect the "Ray" parts and he affects the "Anne" parts.

Few men and women are in a position to do this. But more than physically, a husband needs to bring his wife to his side—into his thinking, his dreams, his plans, his insecurities, his longings. He needs to listen very carefully, as well, to her own thinking and longings. Even though God has designated him the leader, he needs to keep her at his side as a co-equal, as "an heir with him of the gracious gift of life" (1 Pet. 3:7).

Gay Talese, panelist in a discussion on men in a *Vogue Magazine* I read, says something I resonate with, that women don't want a husband who's ambiguous, soft, and easy to push around. He says, "I think we want the more forceful man in ourselves to be alive, and I think we feel that women also want that."[1]

They do.

Oh, when she's falling in love she may think she's looking for someone "sweet"—she calls him "caring"—which usually means that he always gives her her own way. But once married, if she realizes her husband's a creampuff she'll begin to despise him. What she wants most deeply is a true man! She wants him to be vigorous and forceful, to see a goal and go after it.

But he must insist on steering her along with him. Even if she screams and kicks, in her heart she knows she's got hold of a good thing—someone with masculine qualities of aggressiveness and courage, who wants to act and go and seek and do.

I think she's saying, "Be an authentic man—it's what I was dreaming of, all along—but take me with you! I want to be at your side."

---

1. Lorraine Davis, ed., "American Men: What Do They Want?" June 1986, 240.

Woman was taken out of man's side
   to suggest her equality with him—
   not out of his feet to imply inferiority,
      not out of his head to suggest superiority—
      But out of his side, implying companionship,
         under his arm to be protected
         and next to his heart, to be loved.[2]

---

2. Matthew Henry, *Commentary on the Bible* (Peabody, MA: Hendrickson 1991).

15 Reversing the surgery on neutered husbands

Ray again . . .

Strange thing about women. We need them. Adam was incomplete without Eve; he was short one rib. A man needs a woman to recover what he lost!

But he also needs to resist her. Haven't you found that's true—that you need your wife and yet she can bring out the worst in you?

"C'mon," said Eve, God's gift to Adam. "Have some fruit." Everything went downhill from there.

"He ate it," says Genesis 3:6—and he got neutered, castrated, disempowered. He turned wimpy.

> Verse 10: "I was afraid."
> Verse 12: "It was her fault."

He whined. He withdrew. He shrank.
Bernikow describes the attitudes of wimps:

We want independence, but we want a faithful lover.

We want the support of a family, but not its demands.

We want a community, but we don't want to conform to its codes.[1]

Wallace Stegner describes how the lead character in his novel *The Spectator Bird* feels about himself. He's a seventy-year-old man, taking a walk and looking back on his life. He confesses to "absurd tears":

I'm Babbitt, the man who in all his life never did one thing he really wanted to. One of those Blake was scornful of, who controlled their passions because their passions are feeble enough to be controlled. . . . One who would grasp the handle but not the blade. Milquetoast. *Homo castratus.*[2]

Is this you? When you're seventy, might this be your own self-description?

Wimpiness deeply shames a man, maybe to the point of desperation. David Smith lists the results: "suicide, divorce, alcoholism, drugs, murder, rape."[3]

How do you reverse sin's process of slow, inch-by-inch demasculinization? Here's how: Before God, you deal with your personal sins. Then, at least, the possibility of reversal appears. Everything starts with re-establishing a relationship with God.

Adam blew it, and because of him all of us men lost the powers of our manhood and of life itself. But God sent His Son Jesus to redeem all that was lost:

---

1. Louise Bernikow: "Alone: Yearning for Companionship in America," *New York Times Magazine,* 15 August 1982.

2. (Lincoln, NE: University of Nebraska Press, 1976), 209.

3. *Men Without Friends* (Nashville: Thomas Nelson), 18.

> Sin entered the world through one man [Adam],
> and death through sin, and in this way death came to
> all men, because all sinned. . . .
> But the gift is not like the trespass. . . . For if by
> the trespass of the one man, death reigned through that
> one man, how much more will those who receive
> God's abundant provision of grace and of the gift of
> righteousness reign in life through the one man, Jesus
> Christ (Rom. 5:12, 15, 17).

I ask you, man to man: Have you received God's gift through
Christ? First Corinthians 3:11 says that's the foundation, the plat-
form, you stand on—and on it alone you can begin to lift up your
head and stand tall as God's man.

And what is "God's man"? We looked at him in Part II; let
me repeat one paragraph:

> If you're willing to really learn to love Me [says
> God], I promise you these things: the assurance that your
> sins are forever wiped clean, personal joy that explodes
> into motivation and strength, courage to achieve and
> conquer, perspective and wisdom for the darkest times,
> and the feel of a grip of love that never lets you go.

If these things are what you're looking for, then loving God
is your bottom line. And as your personal sin-problem gets dealt
with and you begin to grow in the disciplines of loving Him, God
will be shaping you to become—among other things—your wife's
lover, shelter, advocate, strength, defender, encourager, protector,
and friend.

Actually, your wife may not know at first that she wants this.
In a fallen world, and in a couple's fallen humanity, a guy may resist being all this, and the woman may resist receiving it. Self-love
will build an armor around you; you'll protect yourself instead of
her. Or your wife's self-love will make her put up a shield against
all that you're becoming.

There's only one remedy: keep coming back and back to loving God! In some moments your wife will be a "helper suitable" for you. In others she'll be offering you fruit. Leaning on her or resisting her—neither one is the main thing.

At the judgment you'll stand before God to answer first about your own personal love for Him.

"The main thing is to keep the main thing the main thing."

The main thing, brother—and it will be the finest gift you can bring to your wife—is a solid love-relationship between you and God.

16 God's job description for a married man

<u>Ray again</u> . . .

"God's idea of a good man," writes Anne in *Disciplines of the Home*, "isn't one who wears sweats and talks sports. . . . God asks men . . . to assume leadership, and leadership is basically assuming responsibilities and jobs."[1]

In the Bible you see God's men working hard as they ensured their own family's salvation (Exod. 12:3–4), built places for them to live (Num. 32:16), and fought battles to defend them against enemies (Num. 32:17). Leadership demands work. It ain't easy.

Let's look at seven truths about husband-leadership.

1. Your leadership gets defined in your assuming responsibility for your wife's well-being. You answer to God for that. When Jesus said, "I am the true vine, and my Father is the husbandman" (John 15:1, KJV), you get a sense of what "husband" means; it's like a gardener. I'm to "tend" Anne, to continually look

---

1. (Dallas: Word, 1990), 71.

over her. It's my job to make sure she's nourished and protected so she'll thrive.

2. Husband-leadership is a role God assigns you; it's not a spiritual gift. The Holy Spirit doles out to believers different gifts as He chooses (1 Cor. 12:11), but He expects every husband to lead. Ephesians 5:24 says that your wife is to submit to you (adjust to, adapt to, fit in with you), and it has nothing to do with whether or not you're just naturally a born leader.

When I married Anne I thought I was marrying this sweet, soft, compliant little thing . . . Wo! She turned out to be tough and decisive. I'm naturally a lover, not a fighter, and I was scared to death.

I remember one evening at Princeton when she got too hot to handle. Those were the days when I was a seminary student, and we were trying to parent three babies in a little student apartment on campus. We were tense, we argued, and then she blew like a volcano.

I took a walk.

"God," I prayed, "what have I done? She's not what I expected. I don't know if I can handle her."

It seemed as if the Lord was saying, "You should have known, Ray; you had clues . . . All that steadfastness to follow My will, all that willingness for the mission field . . ."

I prayed, I walked. I asked the Lord to help me lead my wife. Then I walked back into our little apartment.

Since that night we've had many years of married love, and it gets better all the time. I really am the leader, though I lean on her and she loves it. When necessary I can be decisive; when necessary she can be compliant. We fit. And my seeking to learn to handle Anne gradually developed my skills in ministry to handle others, so God could expand my leadership. Now I see better the meaning of 1 Timothy 3:5: "If anyone does not know how to manage his own family, how can he take care of God's church?"

3. Lead her with love. "Husbands, love your wives" (Eph. 5:25). It's God's command, whether you feel like it or not.

And times come when you don't feel like it. Then what? Then you stand fast on your marriage vows. You see, wedding vows are never really just to one other person, putting you into an insignificant little clique of two people. Those vows include all society, to help hold it together and make it work. You've committed yourself not only to your wife but to your world.

Ephesians 5:28 takes this command further: "Husbands ought to love their wives as their own bodies."

Man, what a challenge—especially in these days when male vanity, usually in the name of "health," has reached new highs. Men jog, work out, do aerobics. They quit smoking, avoid red meats, eat salads. They don't "get a haircut" any more, they have it "styled" at many times the price. They wear more jewelry, flashier shirts, tighter pants.

The more money they have, the more their secrets: creaming their faces, coloring their hair, visiting spas, and getting hair transplants and facelifts.

Love their wives as they love their own bodies? Some challenge.

A guy's ego can keep him from loving God, wife, children or others. He's so busy improving himself—his person, his career, his financial portfolio—that he may have little time or thought for anyone outside himself.

And yet God, who created man's precious and valuable sense of Self, tells him to surrender it at the foot of the cross. Then it becomes transformed—not into self-confidence but into confidence in God, which gives him the courage to be what he ought to be.

4. Lead her with Christ's own techniques. Ephesians 5 says to love her the same two ways Christ loves His church.

For one, He gave Himself up totally for the church; He loved her with Calvary love (Eph. 5:25). Love your wife totally—not because of what she is like, but because of *what you are like:* You're God's man, and He's making you righteous.

Secondly, love her by washing her with the Word (Eph. 5:26). Shelter her for her quiet times; see that she gets exposed to

Bible teaching; keep her washed. You'll do yourself a favor: she'll turn out radiant (Eph. 5:27).

5. Leadership involves serving. In Luke your model, Jesus, washed His disciples' feet—and then explained why He did it: "The kings of the Gentiles lord it over them; and you are not to be like that. Instead, the greatest among you should be like the youngest, and the one who rules like the one who serves" (Luke 22:25–26).

And then He made it clear that He was indeed their ruler: "I am among you as one who serves" (Luke 22:27).

Serving is one way—only one—that you show your leadership.

6. Lead her with gracious attentiveness. First Peter 3 says she's the weaker partner (not less important, not of lower quality). "Be considerate, . . . treat [her] with respect" (1 Pet. 3:7). Hey, hear it again—your marriage isn't a business partnership, it's a romance!

How do you court your wife until "death do you part"?

I notice the *New World Dictionary's* definition of the word "court": "To pay respectful or flattering attention to (a person) in order to get something." Yes! You want to get a happy marriage, you want to get happy yourself.

How do you *court* her? Look at the other connected words in the same dictionary:

> You're *court*-eous; you're "polite and gracious."
> You show *court*-esy—"polite, helpful, considerate behavior."
> You're *court*-ly: you're "dignified, polite, elegant." Wow! She'll love it.
> All her life, you engage in *court*-ship: "the act, process, or period of courting or wooing."

Married couples never naturally drift closer together. If you as a husband don't aggressively overcome this drifting by constant courting, the two of you will naturally drift apart.

7. Lead her as your "co-heir"—"heir with you of the gracious gift of life, so that nothing will hinder your prayers" (1 Pet. 3:7). This is awesome. If you treat your wife poorly or ignore her or belittle her, you're putting a roadblock in front of your own personal prayers. You may be His child, but you'll feel like an orphan.

Now, hear this conclusion.

If you "husband" your wife well, you'll suffer. It's a tough job, and sometimes you'll be misunderstood, even falsely accused. You'll love, but the love may not be returned.

But if you "husband" her poorly, you'll suffer more. God will see to that.

"Marriage is a trap," writes Mike Mason:

> It is a trap of pure love. The love is so pure, so intense, that it can be like a big iron gate that clangs shut behind us. And there we are. Imprisoned, of our own free will, in the dungeon of marriage. And the one and only key has been handed over to our partner, a total stranger, to swallow. . . .
>
> When the prison door of love swings shut, the only thing to do is to become more in love than ever. There is just no other way to get out of it.[2]

Loving and discomfort—they'll go together. Loving and embarrassment. Loving and debasement. Loving and self-denial. Loving and self-deprivation.

Loving your wife well will cost you everything. Your very manhood will be forced down on one knee to surrender at the throne of none other than God Himself. The surprise will be that instead of being finally crushed and destroyed, you'll feel on your shoulder the touch of a saber. You'll be told to rise. You'll discover that you've just been knighted.

When a guy says, "I want to be a doctor," he'll face tremendous costs in time, money, effort—all that he has. When another says, "I want to be a concert pianist," he's going to pay a giant price. When you say, "I'm going to love God" and "I'm going to

---

2. *The Mystery of Marriage* (Portland, OR: Multnomah, 1985), 49, 50.

love my wife"—those goals will demand of you a lifetime of disciplines, sometimes to the point of agony.

That's commitment. It means you're going for the gold—and you'll spend anything, sacrifice anything, to win your trophy.

But then—mystery of mysteries—passion for and obedience to God transforms a man's pain into thrill and pleasure; the uncomfortable is touched by the exquisite comfort of God's Holy Spirit. And eventually, maybe when you least expect it, God's grace will lift you to that elevated pedestal, and around your neck will be placed the shining prize.

> May the Lord answer you when you are in distress;
>   may the name of the God of Jacob protect you. . . .
> May he give you the desire of your heart
>   and make all your plans succeed.
> We will shout for joy when you are victorious
>   and will lift up our banners in the name of our God.
> May the Lord grant all your requests (Ps. 20:1, 4, 5).

PART IV

Your Love for Your Children

17 Your father-pattern

<u>Anne writes</u> . . .

Theology always surprises us. We think it must be . . . well, like some large, taxidermist-stuffed animal, to be peered at only by animal lovers who are especially zoology-bent—maybe seminary professors.

One day you happen to brush by theology . . . It's alive!! Its sides heave, quivering to contain enormous power. Its eyes pierce straight to your soul, and as you freeze in fascination, its soft, throaty growl indicates that it's capable of roars that would split boulders.

Swallow that yawn. We're looking at theology, the study of God and God's truths.

For instance, in Ephesians 3:14 Paul writes, "I bow before the Father, from whom all fatherhood derives its name . . ." (NIV marginal reference).

You thought maybe God called Himself "Father" *after you,* to give you an illustration of what He's like? No way. He decided to call *you* "father" *after Him,* to give you an illustration of what you're to be like as a father-copy.

He's the original, the prototype. He's the number-one Father of all things. Out of Him emanates everything—everything—in heaven and on earth.

Among all His creations, His masterpiece (along with the miracle of woman) is the human man/father. And in the father's proportionately small male apparatus God places a tiny quantity of liquid . . . And *voila!* Out of that one human father emanate perhaps millions of human descendants.

. . . Millions? We thought one guy could have only one, two, maybe three kids—or if he's bionic, ten or twenty. Look again at theology! Hebrews 7:10 says that an Old Testament fellow named Levi gave money to Melchizidek. Wait, Levi lived many generations after Melchizidek; how could he give Melchizedek money?

Levi gave Melchizidek money, Hebrews says, because Levi was already in the body of his ancestor Abraham, who gave Melchizidek the money.

Wait a minute. All a man's descendants are already in his body? If we're not mistaken—we tread softly—it looks as if it says that every father carries in his loins his descendants—maybe millions of them—plump ones, skinny ones, musicians, lawmakers, rascals and thieves, woodcarvers, trapeze artists, mathematicians, ventriloquists, people with cleft palates or thick wrists or especially flat ears, butchers, bakers, candlestick makers . . .

And to those descendants are attributed this man's personal actions . . . ?

I think theology just emitted a medium-size roar.

18 Seven fathering characteristics of God

Anne continues . . .

If the heavenly Father is the prototype and human fathers are the copies, how will a dad know how to function unless he copies the original?

See what He's like. Marvel. Ask Him to make you like that, through His empowering Spirit.

1. **The heavenly Father loves His children.** "How great is the love the Father has lavished on us, that we should be called the children of God" (1 John 3:1)!

    And when He loves us, He says so, and He proves it. "This is how God showed his love among us: He sent his one and only Son into the world that we might live through him" (1 John 4:9).

My own daddy said it and expressed it constantly. We had a secret thing when he was holding my hand: he'd give it four short squeezes. That stood for "Do—you—love—me?" I would squeeze back three: "Yes—I—do." He'd squeeze two: "How—much?"

Then I'd go through high drama as I tried to squeeze his hand nearly off his arm.

Or we'd be sitting across a room from each other, and Daddy would point to his cheek and say, "I need something right here." I'd blow him a kiss and he'd catch it in the air, plant it on the spot, and *glow.* We're not just talking when I was six. When I was college age, married, a mother, our rituals went on.

Ray's father loved his five children, but it wasn't in that old-world Swedish culture to express it, and Ray missed those three words "I love you." Years later in the navy, in wartime facing the possibility of death, he wrote his parents a long letter to express his love for them—a business that just seemed long overdue.

When he became a father himself, Ray determined to leave no doubt in the minds of his four kids—two daughters, two sons—how much he loved them. Just the same, as the boys got older Ray didn't kiss and hug them as he had before. Somehow it seemed men don't do that to big boys; you just shake hands.

Then Ray performed a wedding—where the big, burly groom, after the ceremony, went down and kissed not only his mother but his dad, on the cheek.

Ray said it was so great, he wanted to cry. And he came home and told Nels about it and said, "From now on, when I go away on a trip or come back, I'm gonna kiss you until you hit me in the mouth!"

Nels never has. And Ray regularly hugs and kisses his daughters, his daughters-in-law, his sons and his sons-in-law, and easily and always says "I love you" to all the gang.

No child should ever grow up without the security that comes from continually hearing and seeing the proofs of his father's constant love.

2. The heavenly Father provides for His children.

His divine power has given us everything we need for life and godliness (2 Pet. 1:3).

He who did not spare his own Son, but gave him up for us all—how will he not also, along with him, graciously give us all things (Rom. 8:32)?

And yet, look at His style of providing. He doesn't just inundate us with stuff and spoil us. In spite of all God's general assurances, He temporarily withholds when He knows that that's our true need:

> Remember how the Lord your God led you all
> the way in the desert [said Moses to Israel]. . . .
> He humbled you, causing you to hunger and then
> feeding you with manna. . . . Know then in your
> heart that as a man disciplines his son, so the Lord
> your God disciplines you (Deut. 8:2, 3, 5).

Our Father's committed to supply our *needs*—but not our *greeds*.

Donald Barnhouse told a story about getting a letter from his son away in college. He wrote, "Dad, I need money. I spilled acid on my pants in the chemistry lab, and they've got a huge hole. Then a bunch of us are going skiing this weekend and I need ski money."

Dr. Barnhouse sent money for the first request but not the second. He said, "I'm committed to keep my son in pants but not on skis!"

So love provides, but love doesn't overindulge. And often it takes the wisdom of Solomon, doesn't it, to know the difference!

One other thing. Keep in mind the distinction between the heavenly Father's provisions—He who owns all things—and an earthly father's—who doesn't. My own dad could pretty much supply anything within reason; Ray's dad couldn't. Ray earned his own money for everything but food and housing from age twelve on. But he knew his dad was doing all he could do, and it was okay.

3. The heavenly Father guides and instructs His children.

Good and upright is the Lord;
> therefore he instructs sinners in his ways.
He guides the humble in what is right
> and teaches them his way (Ps. 25:8–9).

His will and His way—both are crucial: we need not only to do what He wants us to do, but in the way He wants us to do it.

King David once had a desire to put the ark of God back in its rightful place in Jerusalem; he knew that was God's will. But he hadn't checked out His Word to see His way—how the ark was to be carried. The result was disastrous; lives were even lost (Num. 4:10).

The good father, you see, makes his will and his way known, and then rewards obedience or punishes disobedience. It sounds simple, but it's a heavy commitment, isn't it!

4. The heavenly Father warns His children. He wants to shelter us from harm and trouble, so He fathers us strongly. Listen to His words to Israel:

> Woe to the obstinate children,
>   declares the Lord,
> to those who carry out plans that are not mine, . . .
> who go down to Egypt
>   without consulting me. . . .
> Through a land of hardship and distress,
>   of lions and lionesses,
>   of adders and darting snakes,
> the envoys carry their riches on donkeys' backs,
>   their treasures on the humps of camels,
> to that unprofitable nation,
>   to Egypt, whose help is utterly useless. . . .

[Interesting picture! In self-will, they go through much danger to transport materiel to a place where it doesn't profit.]

> These are a rebellious people, deceitful children,
>   children unwilling to listen to the Lord's instruc-
>   tion (Isa. 30:1, 2, 6, 7, 9).

I wish parents could figure a way to present good and bad choices the dramatic way God did it for Israel; kids love drama. God put half the people on one mountain, Gerizim, and the other half on another close by, Ebal, where they could hear each other. Then Joshua read God's commands from His Word, and the priests pronounced on Mount Gerizim specific blessings if they obeyed, and on Mount Ebal, specific curses if they didn't (Deut. 11:26–30, 27, 28; Josh. 8:30–35). Wow! Stroke of genius.

Never must children forget either the rewards if they obey or the punishments if they sin. And at times every good father has to "lay it on the line" and deal with a child nose-to-nose. God does. Sometimes there's no other way.

God loves us too much to let us get by with the low road. Say the same thing to your kids: "I love you too much to let you get by with this . . ."

Ray told me about a recent delicious experience that he had with Ray, Jr. The two of them had been alone studying the Word, and then they got down on their knees to pray. Ray says he won't forget our son's strong intercessions for his four children: "Lord, I will not give up any of my children to the world—" and he began to weep. "Lord, I refuse to let them go. Keep them in Your gracious hand. O God, I love them so much! I insist on their being all-out for You." Grandfather and father wept together.

Father, be a man of desperate prayer for your children! The world, the flesh, and the devil are all after their souls, minds, and bodies—but God is greater, and there is no power like overcoming prayer!

And express your concerns. Ray told our kids dozens of times, "I'm not asking you to be Christians who are nice, polite, and harmless. I long for you to live or die for Jesus! He didn't go through all of Calvary for you to turn out gutless and mediocre!"

5. The heavenly Father affirms His children.
[You are] God's chosen people, holy and dearly loved . . . (Col. 3:12).

[He] has qualified you to share in the inheritance of the saints . . . (Col. 1:12).

He who began a good work in you will carry it on to completion . . . (Phil. 1:6).

I've written a book on how to affirm the children: *Children Are Wet Cement*, published by Fleming H. Revell. (See the listing in the front of this book.) I hope you'll read it.

Kids never get too much delight from their parents. Except for the moments when you're disciplining them, let them be your constant joy—and say so!

I still have a little warm place in my heart from a memory of when I was about ten. The odometer on our car read "6006," and Daddy said, "Look, Anne, the mileage number is symmetrical." "No, it's not," I said. "To be symmetrical, one of the sixes would have to be backward."

Daddy went crazy. He raved about what a perceptive eye I had, and he said I might grow up to be a great artist, and he told his friends about it in front of me.

That affirmation kept my motor running smoothly for a long time.

6. The heavenly Father protects His children.

[Love] always protects (1 Cor. 13:7).

You are my hiding place," David sang (Ps. 32:7).

As the mountains surround Jerusalem,
    so the Lord surrounds his people
    both now and forevermore (Ps. 125:2).

Many people these days are arguing that the ancient roles of men as protectors and women as the protected must be scrapped if the sexes are now considered equal. Scripture says it differently: they are and always have been equal (Galations 3:28 says, "There is neither . . . male nor female, for you are all one in Christ Jesus") but that their roles are different. (The differences have nothing to do with superiority or inferiority.)

If fathers are to take their cues from the heavenly Father, they do indeed watch over and protect their wives and children.

7. The heavenly Father never abandons His children.

Never will I leave you [He says],
    never will I forsake you (Heb. 13:5)!

> The eyes of the Lord are on the righteous
> > and his ears are attentive to their cry (Ps. 34:15).

> He will not let your foot slip—
> > he who watches over you will not slumber. . . .
> The Lord will keep you from all harm—
> > he will watch over your life (Ps. 121:3, 7).

Oh, what security that truth gives every believer!

And what security gets built into a child who trusts that *Father is there.*

The surveys are frightening on what happens to the emotions of children whose parents divorce. Many are unable to relate meaningfully to an adult all the rest of their lives, for fear of being abandoned over again. Their true hope is to come to know deeply the love of God, and be able to say, "Though my father and mother forsake me, the Lord will receive me" (Ps. 27:10).

This is indeed the assurance from God's own mouth:

> Can a mother forget the baby at her breast
> > and have no compassion on the child she has
> > borne?
> Though she may forget,
> > I will not forget you (Isa. 49:15)!

The child, on the other hand, may be the one to leave, or to forget. The prodigal son walked out on the father, and the father let him go. But did he forget him? Listen, that father's waiting was so alert, he saw him returning from a long way off—and ran to receive him back again. And he threw a party (Luke 15:11–24)!

"Never will I leave you," says the heavenly Father. Dad, you can't say that; war, sickness, death may separate. Oh, how crucial, then, for your family to be well-bonded to the original, perfect Father—the One who "lives in us and will be with us forever" (2 John 2).

19 Law versus grace

More from Anne . . .

There's so much to parenting that's tricky, isn't there! There are so many situations that don't have any easy answers.

That's why we must draw closer and closer to the heavenly Father, through His Word and through prayer, to catch the heart-beat, the spirit, of what parenting's really about.

Do you notice that most marriage and family books are full of *lists?* In the first place, lists look great on a page—they leave lots of white space. Besides that, most parents really go for six commands for shaping up Junior and fourteen commands for relating to their spouses . . . "Just tell us in black and white what to do!"

But law-oriented parenting tends to make driven parents and kids. It substitutes duties and techniques and activities for relationships, the greatest need of Mother as well as Father. There's not even much *time* to look deep into their little psyches and, with an arm around them, seek to figure them out.

Endless lists of man-made rules say, "Here's the way to control your children; just have a law to cover every situation." There's no ambiguity; there's no space; there are no questions; they're in

a closed system. And it may take years to discover that in that system the kids can't breathe. Eventually, for air, they may burst so
far out of the family, you don't see them again till they're forty-two.

Is your family law-oriented or grace-oriented?

You know how the heavenly Father wants His family to be;
He wrote the whole book of Galatians to make it clear:

> All who rely on observing the law are under a
> curse. . . . Christ redeemed us from the curse of the
> law. . . . Now that faith has come, we are no longer
> under the supervision of the law. . . . Stand firm,
> then, and do not let yourselves be burdened again by
> a yoke of slavery (Gal. 3:10, 13, 25; 5:1).

Law-oriented families produce perfectionists. Their speech
is full of do's and don'ts and oughts and shoulds. Couples with
their first babies, or the first child of that sex, are almost always
law-oriented; this is going to be the perfect child! So, says Kevin
Leman in his *Birth Order Book,* the firstborn ends up—

> perfectionistic, reliable, conscientious, a list maker, well
> organized, critical, serious, scholarly, . . . goal ori-
> ented, an achiever, self-sacrificing, a people pleaser,
> conservative, a supporter of law and order, a believer
> in authority and ritual, legalistic, loyal, self reliant.[1]

All those qualities aren't bad. I hope they're not; I'm a firstborn,
myself! But I know the pressure, the uptightness, the "must" and
"ought" of it, too. We firstborns try too hard. And if we don't toe
the mark we lie, we cover up. Oh, do I need my last-born Ray!

So I'm getting afraid of all those lists. One-two-three steps
toward perfection keep people ashamed. Onward and onward
they toil, never perfectly satisfying either the law or themselves.

Ray and I visited a law-oriented home a while ago. The house
was perfect. The refreshments were perfect. The parents were

---

1. (Old Tappan, NJ: Fleming H. Revell, 1985), 61.

perfect. The five children were perfect. They played the piano. They recited verses. They were all The Seven of the Frozen Smile. Everybody sat upright on chairs. When we left everybody went to the window, and everybody waved little Queen Elizabeth waves.

I wonder if any of them will ever have the courage to be real people.

You know about the family that had a mother cat and four kittens, and the kitchen outside wall had not one cat-hole but five. The woman explained why: "When I say scat, I mean SCAT!"

You get the picture. It just all gets to be too much.

A law-oriented boss chews out his employee. The employee can't answer back so he goes home and chews out his wife. She chews out the teenage son. He kicks the dog. The dog bites the cat. The cat scratches the baby. The baby pulls the doll's head off.

It makes a miserable world.

We could say, "Well, the law beats drugs and teenage sex and . . ."

But God says, "I show you a more excellent way" (1 Cor. 12:31, KJV).

> The Lord is compassionate and gracious,
>   slow to anger, abounding in love.
> He will not always accuse,
>   nor will he harbor his anger forever.
> He does not treat us as our sins deserve (Ps. 103:8–10).

Our response? The verse following: "Praise the Lord, O my soul" (Ps. 103:22)!

Get inside the skins of your kids; try to feel what they're feeling. Sin is a terrible burden; they are miserable. Sin is the mystery of the ages, isn't it! You're caught in it; they're caught in it. However you react, include some grieving!

I feel so sorry for Job with his so-called "friends." He didn't need advice; he still had all those empty chairs around the table. He was suddenly broke. He needed a fresh sense of the love of God, and a lifting, comforting nearness of the love of other people.

In your family, when sin increases, let grace increase all the more (Rom. 5:20). Of course, punish; but beyond all that, be kind! Like the rest of us, children need kindness.

Jesus was so kind, so encouraging. He said—

of Mary, "She has done a beautiful thing."
to Zacchaeus, "I want to have lunch with you."
to the Roman centurion, "I haven't seen such faith in all Israel."
To Peter, "I have prayed for you . . .

Kindness goes a long way. Ask God continually to make you a kind person: Kind to your wife. Kind to your children. Kind to others.

I've heard that this was said by Mother Teresa: "Kind words can be short and easy to speak, but their echoes are truly endless."

One final word: Don't only dispense grace—receive it too.

You're painfully aware, aren't you, of your weaknesses, mistakes, goofs as a father. You may blame yourself for too much.

Our heavenly Father has rebellious kids; that doesn't mean He's a bad father.

My people would not listen to me (He says in Psalm
81:11, 12);
Israel would not submit to me.
So I gave them over to their stubborn hearts
to follow their own devices.

God gives every human being a will of his own, to obey or to disobey. If your children are at this moment rebellious, it doesn't necessarily mean you're a bad parent.

Every newborn enters the world as a combination of inherited genes: this from his dad, this from his mom, this from his grandfather Albert, this from his great-grandmother Suzanna—but more. He also has a mystery ingredient all his own. He comes into the world with his own Self. He inherited it from nobody, and nobody has it but him.

And then as he grows up—with his own individual Self, with that will which is his personal property, he weighs all the input, and he chooses right or he chooses wrong. God gives each human the self-dignity of his own choices.

That means, if your kids turn out great, you can't take all the credit.

And if they turn out poorly, you can't take all the blame.

20 Fathering daughters

Ray writes . . .

They say that once you have a child, from then on your heart walks around outside your body.

Oh, my two girls! . . . In their growing-up years I used to say, "Any fella who comes around and tries to take away one of my daughters, I'm gonna pop him in the mouth."

Dads have no problem bonding with their daughters. A son is a potential rival (so the psychologists say), but a daughter is his baby princess and that's that.

Anne and I worked at keeping all our kids close. Sherry and Margie were each born in the wintertime and could have started into first grade before they were six. We deliberately kept them out of preschool and then started them late into formal schooling, to give them as much time as possible just being exposed to two parents.

They particularly had my full attention, as well as Anne's, on Mondays, my days off; often on that day we went out of town for some special adventure. The kids grew up with family picnics, dancing Looby-loo, playing family games . . . Daily we read the Bible and prayed together, sometimes singing hymns, too, or memorizing Scripture.

"Make the most of every opportunity," says Ephesians 5:16. The days of child-raising go by so fast; mold the clay while it's wet!

The girls' teenage years got very busy, and Anne and I began to feel the need for more togetherness with them. Saturdays and Sundays were two of my busiest days, so we got permission from the schools to take them out on occasional Mondays, one at a time, just to be with us. Their teachers were sympathetic and cooperative. Sherry, our conscientious firstborn, was sometimes hesitant to miss, anyway, but Margie would beg to go every Monday of her flibbertigibbet life.

A daughter, especially as she grows, is, to a father, a mystery, a fascination, a wonder. A son he can understand better; he's been there. And when I was little, sisters were just playmates and rivals. But a daughter—! Oh, a daughter!

Daughters beginning to sprout are tenderly comical. When one of mine would arrive at the breakfast table with a new lumpy hairdo hanging over one eye and maybe the nose, I'd plead, "Come on, I need to see your beautiful face."

Then the hair would get skinned back, exposing painted eyes, greasy lipstick, and face makeup right to the jaw line—and behind the jaw line, a dirty neck.

Just the same, here was my own flesh and blood, maturing into womanhood with all its magical powers and allure. I watched Sherry and Margie metamorphosing into young ladies, and with all their giggles and tears, I marveled to myself, "What hath God wrought!"

And yes, it's true, I was nervous over accepting Walt and John, their husbands, into my heart. It's like a father's turning over his priceless Stradivarius violin to a thousand-pound gorilla. The wedding, no matter how happy it's supposed to be, strikes you as a terrible mistake.

Walt and John are both remarkable men, and I grudgingly admit both daughters have blossomed and strengthened and matured under their wise handling. Even today when I have one-on-one lunches with Sherry or Margie, I see their joy.

But I can say there's a special love affair that goes on between a father and his daughters—a sweet mystique, an unexplainable mystery in the dynamics of the relationships. It's true; it's wonderful; and I leave it at that.

Yes, now my two daughters are grown women.

They're not like my two sons, whose hearts I can probe at will because they're my best friends, and friends freely share. Sherry and Margie are best friends, too, but it's different—they're women. They each belong to another man. I can go only so far, and then it's hands off.

I love them deeply, and I know they love me. I reach across the table and take that hand and say "I love you," and a ton of "I love you's" comes back. But I love them with respect; I know my limits. There's only one woman in the world I can probe and probe, to know with ever-deepening knowledge: that's Anne. She's my own woman, my very own, my only woman.

Anne recently had lunch with Sherry and Margie to talk about this father-daughter thing. May I expose my heart to you by reading from Anne's notes? I'm embarrassed to do it, but here are some comments:

> MARGIE: "When we see each other Daddy is always interested in me; I feel validated. And he's often self-exposing, which makes me feel that I'm valued by him."
>
> SHERRY: "Feminism is personally a puzzle to me. I've never needed it; I've never felt a lack. Dad has always made me feel I had much to contribute."
>
> MARGIE: "Daddy affirms my femininity. He compliments me on how I look; he treats me gently. The guys, he pals with—but me, he treats as a little fragile. It's nice . . .
>
> "John says when I talk to Daddy on the phone my voice changes. I don't talk adult-to-adult, mind-to-mind; my affectionate self speaks."
>
> SHERRY: "A daughter gets from her mother all the mothering stuff. But she gets from her father how she feels about her own worth.

"By the very way Dad treated you, Mom—using you, for instance, to research extra sermon material—I got the idea that women have important contributions to make. And now he uses me, too, in writing projects, and I love it.

"I remember walking around the block with Dad, and he told me, 'Think big about your life. Have big dreams! Have God-sized expectations!'"

What a good fathering job Philip the evangelist must have done! He traveled and preached, but he must have taken time to be with his girls, teaching them theology and instilling in them confidence that God could powerfully use them. Look at the result in Acts 21:9: "[Philip] had four unmarried daughters who prophesied."

As your daughters grow up, Father, release them to fly as far as God wants them to fly. And give them the gift of continual, behind-the-scenes prayer.

And then whenever the occasion demands, pray to Christ as did Jairus, that concerned father, "Please come and put your hands on [my daughter], so that she will be healed, and live" (Mark 5:23).

The special love between father and daughter needs to have upon it always the benediction of God.

21 Fathering sons

Ray continues . . .

Robert Bly writes, "We know that our society produces a plentiful supply of boys but seems to produce fewer and fewer men. . . .

"We have no idea at all how to produce men, and we let it all happen unconsciously while we look away to Wall Street and hope for the best."[1]

Sad commentary. Anne in her book *Children Are Wet Cement* gives a parenting plan which would be an antidote for the looking-away-to-Wall-Street mode:

1. Become all that you should be in Christ;

2. Keep your child close to you until what you are has been transmitted.

---

1. *Iron John* (Redding, MA: Addison-Wesley, 1990), 180.

This puts an awesome responsibility on parents, but it's how God grows and stretches both generations. "Follow my example," wrote Paul (Phil. 3:17; 2 Thess. 3:7). "Do what you have seen me do," said Abimelech (Judg. 9:48). "Watch me," said Gideon. "Follow my lead. . . . Do exactly as I do" (Judg. 7:17).

Fathers transmit their own style to their sons, consciously or otherwise. How many times has a remote father caused his boys to grow up feeling that to be masculine means to be remote! And then they think Christianity must be for women and sissies, because it discourages remoteness!

"Follow my example." "Do as I do." I can still see little Buddy (Ray, Jr.), about two, swaggering around in my old sailor hat. Anne said that especially from the back, his blond head and rolling gait and pigeon toes were an exact reproduction. Scary.

Your sons pick up your goods and bads, both. Look, for instance, at Abraham, and then at his son Isaac, a generation later:

> [Abraham] built an altar there to the Lord (Gen. 12:7).

> Isaac built an altar there and called on the name of the Lord (Gen. 26:25).

> The Lord had said to Abram, "Leave your country." . . . So Abram left (Gen. 12:1, 4).

> The Lord appeared to Isaac and said, "Do not go down to Egypt." . . . So Isaac stayed (Gen. 26:2, 6).

The "old block" obeys God; the "chip" does the same.

But the "old block" gets in the habit of lying about his beautiful wife—and what do you expect will follow?

> [Abram] said to his wife Sarai, . . . "Say you are my sister" (Gen. 12:11, 13).

> For a while [Abraham] stayed in Gerar, and there Abraham said of his wife Sarah, "She is my sister . . ." (Gen. 20:1, 2).

> When the men of that place asked [Isaac] about
> his wife, he said, "She is my sister . . ." (Gen. 26:7)!

This tendency to propagate, whether we like it or not, means staying on our knees! It means seeking to love God first, and then we're in a position to reproduce our God-oriented selves.

Become all you should be. . . .

Stay close to your child until he also becomes. . . .

There's something tough about moving in close to little boys. They never flush the toilet, brush their teeth, or put in their shirttails. They knock over everything they pass, especially if it's breakable. Their faces and hands are always dirty, and they love to spit, burp, and jump on things. No wonder child psychiatrist Ross Campbell says that six-year-old boys get only one-sixth as much hugging and kissing as six-year-old girls.[2] "Sticks and snails and puppy-dog tails, that's what little boys are made of." It's understandable.

Son, come back when you're thirty.

But that's too late.

Joel Weldon says the Chinese plant a seed of the Chinese bamboo tree. Then they water and fertilize it for four years without seeing any results.

But then—

> Sometime during the course of the fifth year, in
> a period of approximately six weeks, the Chinese bam-
> boo tree grows roughly ninety feet.
>
> The question is, Did it grow ninety feet in six
> weeks or did it grow ninety feet in five years? The ob-
> vious answer is that it grew ninety feet in five years,
> because had they not applied water and fertilizer each
> year there would have been no Chinese bamboo tree.[3]

---

2. Quoted by Zig Ziglar, *Raising Positive Kids in a Negative World* (New York: Ballantine Books, 1985), 179.

3. Ibid., 31.

But this is really a poor illustration, first, because most little boys aren't that obnoxious (*you* weren't, Bud and Nels—honest), and second, because you don't care for them through those early years and see nothing at all happen.

Plenty happens. And there are many rewarding moments along the way.

There is a special father-pride in raising a son because the dad identifies. You love to see him do what you did; even more, to see him do what you never did or couldn't do. There is the conflict inside you of tremendous delight over his accomplishments and, on the other hand, of competition. (He feels the same conflicting pressures—to please you and yet be better than you.)

There's not the mystery, though, that there is in relating to daughters. In your son you see yourself. You understand each other, and you don't need to spell it out.

And you long for him to do well because he's an extension of you, your alter ego. Like self-love, son-love goes very deep. How much Solomon must have loved his boys, to write as he did to them with such thoughtfulness and passion:

> The proverbs of Solomon, son of David . . . (Prov. 1:1).
>
> [Pride in lineage! It's how we've developed surnames like "Johnson" and "Robertson" and "Jacobson." Solomon could have called himself "Solomon Davidson."]
>
> Listen, my son, to my father's instruction . . . (Prov. 1:8).
>
> My son, do not forget my teaching . . . (Prov. 3:1).
>
> My son, pay attention . . . (Prov. 5:1).

He talks turkey to him about wisdom, finances, work, wayward women, discipline—what cuts life short and brings misery, and what gives long life, success, and happiness. He longs for his son to have the best!

(In my caring so much, I could pontificate and blow it. After one of my impassioned speeches, teenage Bud replied with,

"The wisdom of the universe has just spoken." I deserved that. I tried afterward to learn to calm down.)

Caring communication is an art in itself. My beloved mentor Tom Bunn, a godly, wise older attorney, said to me once, "Ray, it's not enough to be right; you must be rightly understood." And Zig Ziglar says, "If you don't listen to your children's problems, they won't listen to your solutions."[4]

Anne's dad said it best of all. When I was a new father I asked his advice on raising children. He said, "Ray, treat them like real people."

Once when Ray, Jr. had grown to adulthood, I asked him what had helped him most in my fathering him. He said, "When I was nine years old and you were considering moving from New York to take a church in California, and you asked my advice."

Wow, I did something right.

Writes Gordon Dalbey, "When a boy reaches puberty, filled with the powerful physical stirrings of his emerging manhood, the father's role becomes critical."[5]

He needs to bond with you, Dad, more than ever before. At this point he mustn't continue a dependence on his mother which would detract from bonding well with a wife later on. He needs to relate to you as the image of what he soon will be—and to enjoy it!

Should there be some kind of Christian "Bar Mitzvah" ceremony? My friend Ken had one for each of his boys, formalized occasions to which family and many friends were invited. They were very meaningful, and to the sons, I'm sure, never to be forgotten.

But the payoff comes when a father and son can move together into an adult relationship. The competition has dissolved forever, and what remains is delicious friendship.

It's hard to describe the sheer joy of father-son and father-daughter relationships that are in Christ!

---

4. *Raising Positive Kids,* 165.

5. *Healing the Masculine Soul* (Dallas: Word, 1988), 132.

At least once a week I'm on the phone with Ray, Jr., our theologian son. The one calling may say, "I was lonely for you and just wanted to hear your voice. I'm so proud of you. Tell me what's going on." The older we grow, it seems, the closer we become.

Our youngest, Nels, age twenty-eight, and I go out for dinners together. We talk about his lovely Heather and their new little son, Bradford; we talk about our desires, angers, purposes, disappointments, what we're weak in, what we struggle with, what we're scared of, our risks, our secret thrills . . .

Genesis 44:30 says that Jacob's life was "closely bound up with [his] boy's life." I understand that very well.

One more thing.

Every boy needs heroes. Hopefully your son will basically see you as a hero, even through your weaknesses and the bad memories of your goofs.

But take him beyond yourself. Give him Jesus—from birth on. Later give him Washington and Lincoln and Teddy Roosevelt and Winston Churchill. Give him Jonathan Goforth and Hudson Taylor and Jim Elliot. Give him Billy Graham and Charles Colson.

What makes a hero? Painstaking thought. Self-imposed discipline. Black periods, grief. Passion. Energy. Courage in confronting risk.

Maybe someday your son will be a hero.

<u>Anne's song</u>

God, make my son a tree!
So tall and fair is he—
    But height and form are not enough,
    And outward looks can be a bluff;
God, make him giant-tall inside,
With yearnings only satisfied
    To stretch and strive,
    To reach and rise
Up to the skies!

God, make my son a stone
Upon a beach alone.
    Though wind and waves may pound and beat
    And claw the soil about his feet,
O God, imbed his mind and heart
With deepness, quiet and apart,
    That he, though bound
    By storms around,
May stand his ground!

God, see this fine young son.
And what else should be done?
    Carve him, and shape to some good form,
    Sincere and useful, wise and warm . . .
O God, it's hard to let him go,
And yet I know it's better so.
    God, see my son,
    my lovely son!
I give him to
    the world and You.

Anne Ortlund

22 Blessing your household

Ray continues . . .

When I was newly living in Pasadena I remember reading 2 Samuel 6:20, how King David "returned home to bless his household." And I thought, "That's what I'd like to do, every evening when I return home."

So for many years, late in the afternoon as I drove homeward through the streets of Pasadena, I'd come to a certain lamppost. In my mind, I would hang all my problems on that lamppost. Then I'd drive on home and into the garage, asking God to make me a blessing that evening to my household.

Dad, in your household situation you're the point man.

When your children get to be three or four and begin to be curious about abstract subjects like God, be watching for the time when they can make the all-important step of receiving Jesus as Savior. Be praying for the Holy Spirit to illumine their minds and open their hearts. Our children were each around four or five when they took the actual step, and each time either Anne or I was on the scene.

Five-year-old Nels was sitting between his mother and "Uncle Harold" (Harold Peck) at midweek prayer meeting. After a time of prayer Nels poked Anne and said, "Mamma, I just asked Jesus to come into my heart." Then he turned and told Uncle Harold. As soon as the meeting was over he came up and told me.

When we got home from church that night, we wrote in the front of my Bible that Nels had received the Lord on that date, and Nels signed his name. It was a time of great joy!

As with each of the other children, it made an immediate difference. Nels wasn't suddenly perfect, but in dealing with him we now had an Ally: the Holy Spirit within him was encouraging him to go the way we were leading.

And that first week the Spirit led him to tell strategic people that he'd accepted Jesus: the grocer at the supermarket and Anne's hairdresser—two people Anne was prayerfully witnessing to at the time.

"Let the little children come to me," says Jesus, "and do not hinder them" (Matt. 19:4). Indeed, help them!

There's the foundation of the household: Christ. Pray and work that every member be saved and strongly connected to Him.

23 Sheltering your household

<u>Ray continues</u> . . .

Move the zoom lens back, and let's see God's strategy for the family as a unit of society.

J. D. Unwin, British social anthropologist, spent seven years studying the births and deaths of eighty civilizations—seeing what made them swell to vitality, what made them die. One of his conclusions was this:

> The energy which holds a society together is sexual in nature. When a man is devoted to one woman and one family, he is motivated to build, save, protect, plan and prosper on their behalf.
>
> However, when his sexual interests are dispersed and generalized, his effort is invested in the gratification of sensual desires.[1]

---

1. Quoted by James Dobson, *Dare to Discipline* (Wheaton, IL: Tyndale House, Regal Books, 1970) 161.

And Dr. Unwin said,

> Any human society is free either to display great
> energy or to enjoy sexual freedom; the evidence is that
> they cannot do both for more than one generation.[2]

God knew this awesome truth very well when He wrote,
through Paul, rules for father-models in the local church:

> He must manage his own family well and see that
> his children obey him with proper respect. . . .
> A deacon [also] must be the husband of but one
> wife and must manage his children and his household
> well (1 Tim. 3:4, 12).

This was written when the young church was sprouting in the
midst of decaying Rome. Sexual sins and sensuality were everywhere around, and these strong, simple words, the way to health
and life, were in stark contrast to the Christians' social environment
of sickening and death.

The young church was in the world, but the world had not
yet seeped into the church.

Our present world is often compared with Rome in its last
days. The difference for the church is, the ocean is pouring into
our boat! All the sins of the surrounding world are now flooding
into our churches, our families, our lifestyles, our thinking, our
opinions.

Who are the fathers who will guard their own households
and keep out the sea? Who are the ones brave enough to protect their own families and say, "God helping me, we're going to
follow the way of health and life"? Or to say like Joshua to his
degenerating society, "If serving the Lord seems undesirable to
you, then choose for yourself this day whom you will

---

2. Ibid.

serve. . . . But as for me and my house, we will serve the Lord" (Josh. 24:15)?

Never forget that you and your household are "strangers and pilgrims" in a foreign land; you're set down in the midst of a culture that's hell-bent for destruction. You and your family are to be "in it but not of it."

Father, put blood on your doorpost (Exod. 12:7 ff.). Mark your household for God.

In a way, you're like the Hebrews living as exiles in corrupt Babylon, far from their real home. To them Jeremiah wrote, "Build houses and settle down; plant gardens and eat what they produce. Marry and have sons and daughters. . . . Increase in number there; do not decrease" (Jer. 29:5–6).

We must live, we must function—but we must keep separate. We settle down, we build, we reproduce—but we must stay pure. We must tell our kids, "Look, we're not like the world. We belong to Jesus. And we marry only our own kind—others who also belong to Jesus."

Furthermore, Jeremiah also told the Jewish exiles, "Seek the peace and prosperity of the city [in] which I have [placed] you. . . . Pray to the Lord for it, because if it prospers, you too will prosper" (Jer. 29:7).

Or, as Paul wrote to Timothy, "I urge, then, . . . that requests, prayers, intercession and thanksgiving be made for everyone— for kings and all those in authority, that we may live peaceful and quiet lives in all godliness and holiness" (1 Tim. 2:1–2).

Pray for your country and its leaders not only because they need it, but because you also will get the benefit.

But no one can battle for your own family but you. The task today is for men who are warriors. This is where, warrior of God, your battle line is drawn: around your own family. And no one else can do it for you.

Look at the functions of God's men in the Bible. Israel was the model society, and here was its hierarchy:

1. One nation;

2. Within the nation, twelve tribes;

3. Within the tribes, clans;

4. Within the clans, families;

5. Within each family, one man, the father.

When the Israelites were called together, each father took his place at the front of his family, to answer for his family's sins (Josh. 7:14–15), and to protect his family's rights and needs (Josh. 21:1–2). Nobody could stand there but him.

There are some things a man has to do all by himself.

He has to blow his own nose.

He has to make his own love.

And he has to defend and protect his own family.

24 Transmitting your heritage

<u>Ray again</u> . . .

Individuals make your family. But in a more permanent way, your family makes the individuals within it.

Get grandfather's portrait up on the wall; it can be a powerful incentive to right living. Our daughter Margie is great at this: ancestral pictures are everywhere, and John and Margie's kids know where they came from, what stuff they're made of, and what's expected of their generation.

What if your family doesn't have a good past? Then you be the starter of the good family; you become the ancestor whose portrait will someday be on the wall!

Says a good father, according to Psalm 78,

> O my people, hear my teaching;
> > listen to the words of my mouth. . . .
> I will utter things hidden from of old—
> > things we have heard and known,
> > things our fathers have told us.

> We will not hide them from their children;
> > we will tell the next generation
> the praiseworthy deeds of the Lord,
> > his power, and the wonders he has done. . . .
> so the next generation would know them,
> > even the children yet to be born,
> > and they in turn would tell their children (Ps.
> > 78:1–6).

What happens when the chains of transfer are broken? Charles Colson says this:

> When radical individualism fragments the family, it fragments the transmission of manners and morals from one generation to the next. . . .
> No matter how we try to compensate, it is nearly impossible for those left drifting at this stage to catch up later. . . . Unable to hand down our moral heritage, we raise generation after generation of increasingly rude, lawless, and culturally retarded children.[1]

Consider the alternative.

Charles Hodge (1797–1878) was an influential theologian, the dominant professor of Princeton Theological Seminary in his day and author of a still-studied three-volume systematic theology. He was involved in the training of about three thousand young pastors.

Dr. Hodge's study there at Princeton was part of his home and had two doors. One door led to the inner hall of the house, the other to the out-of-doors. His two sons and their friends, and later his grandchildren, used his study as Grand Central Station, racing at will from indoors to outdoors and back—while Dr. Hodge studied, wrote, prepared class lectures, and graded papers.

Says his biographer,

---

1. *Against the Night* (Ann Arbor: Servant, 1989), 127–28.

They were at every age and at all times allowed free access to him. If they were sick, he nursed them. If they were well, he played with them. If he were busy, they played about him.[2]

How did these boys turn out? The older son first served as a missionary in India, then as a pastor and teacher in the United States, and finally joined Princeton's faculty, succeeding his father when the older man died. He also authored *Outlines of Theology*, which is still being published.

The second son also pastored for several years and then taught on the Princeton faculty for the rest of his life. And his own son became the third generation of Hodges to teach at Princeton—all three holding strongly to the authority of Scripture in a time of intense pressures to shift to doctrinal liberalism.

Reuben A. Torrey, during the first quarter of the twentieth century one of the great preachers on both sides of the Atlantic, had five children. One daughter died when she was nine. His oldest daughter never married, taught twenty years at Wheaton College, and was known as a great woman of prayer. The second daughter, Blanche, devoted her life to raising her five children. One of her daughters married a coach at Wheaton College, and the two of them ministered to young people many years at Word of Life camp in Schroon Lake.

Another daughter and her husband were missionaries in Costa Rica, another daughter and husband in the Congo (now Zaire). The oldest daughter of this clan, R. A. Torrey's great-granddaughter, married Dallas Cowboy ex-coach Tom Landry.

Dr. Torrey's only son served forty-six years as a missionary in China and Korea. Three of his children were missionaries in China, Japan, and Korea. A daughter has written several books, is a conference speaker, and has a radio program.

---

2. Russ Pullman, "The Legacy of Faithful of Parents" (from an article in Ligonier Ministries *Tabletalk Magazine*, July 1992).

Among R. A. Torrey's great-grandsons are four ministers and one preparing for the ministry.

Anne's own father, my father-in-law Joe Sweet, a general in the U.S. Army, and her mother Betty taught Bible classes on all the army posts where they were stationed in their thirty-some years of military life, and then for twenty more years in his second career as a publisher.

Beyond the faithful family devotions every night and bedside prayers, Joe Sweet spent lots of time talking and singing with his children and grandchildren. There were endless, outlandish "Cowboy Joe" stories, made up in his head as he went along, and funny folk-type songs he had heard as a boy. He loved to go on walks with them, he held their hands, he looked in their eyes, he listened to whatever they said and took them very seriously.

A while back the Sweet clan had a family reunion at Cape Cod. Everybody came, all forty-seven of us—everyone except Joe and Betty, now in heaven, and their only son Bob, a pilot whose plane went down in World War II, also in heaven. Otherwise, all Joe Sweet's children, grandchildren, and great-grandchildren were at the reunion. All forty-seven, except the babies, are active Christians. We spent part of our time recalling the past, the older ones mostly supplying what the young ones needed to know. We spent part of the time surveying the present, with reports, testimonies, and prayers for each other's lives. We spent the last part envisioning the future, praying especially for pregnant mothers and pastors and others launching into new ministries around the world. And we dedicated ourselves as a family again to the Lord Jesus.

If Dad Sweet were alive, he'd say, "To Him be the glory."

What can you ask God for, Father, to create the kind of family life that transmits truths, purposes, and a high quality of living from one generation to the next? Ask Him for time, money, and a sense of identity.

1. Ask Him for time. There's no substitute. Everything takes time: Family picnics. Hikes. Projects. Ball games. Occasional extra-long family meals. Bible reading and prayers. Table games. Maybe music together. Jokes and being silly . . . It all takes time. Said Prince Otto von Bismarck (1815–1898), "You can do anything with children if you only play with them."[3]

2. Ask God for money. It takes plenty, doesn't it, to raise a family! But years from now, when they're settled, they won't remember whether you had a new jacket or not; they'll remember the amusement park, the train ride, the circus, the vacation visiting Washington, D.C. . . .

3. Ask God for a family identity. Our friend Dick designed a family crest and put it over the fireplace. He wants his five to be proud of their family individuality.

We often told our kids, especially in their teen years, "We don't care what the others are doing; you're not the others! You're Ortlunds, and this is what the Ortlunds do. When you're parents someday, then feel free to change the rules—but for now, for us, this is how we are, and this is what we do."

The interesting thing is, now a generation later, they have all basically raised their kids as they were raised. The transmission has happened.

"The most crucial thing we can do," says Charles Colson, "is also the quietest—and the most difficult: We must strengthen our commitment to model strong families ourselves, to live by godly priorities. . . ."[4]

Godly priorities don't necessarily just make rules—"You can't smoke and you can't chew, and you can't go with girls who do"— godly priorities make joy! At any given moment, Dad, you may not realize it, but most of all, you're passing on the blessing of life—real, abundant life.

Chuck Colson goes on, "Even huge societal problems are solved one person at a time."[5]

---

3. Laurence J. Peter, *Peter's Quotations* (New York: Bantam Books, 1977), 79.

4. *Against the Night,* 128.

5. Ibid.

Indulge me a few final comments on fathering:

> If I could do it all over again . . .
> > I'd like to make more mistakes.
> I'd relax. I'd limber up.
> > I would be sillier than I was the first time.
> I would take fewer things seriously.
> > I'd let them take more chances.
> > I'd let them have more fun.
> I'd let them eat fewer carrots and more ice cream.
> > Maybe I'd have more actual troubles,
> > but I'd have fewer imaginary ones.

PART V

Your Love
for Others

25 Woman's lament

<u>Anne begins</u> . . .

How is it that you men work so much harder on the technical fix than the human fix? Why do you somehow tend to think of yourselves, anyway, as first of all technicians? Ultimately it actually kills you.

Believe me, we women are so concerned! We look around the restaurants and resort hotels, and we see how many older single women are trying to keep each other company . . . We look, and we wonder, will we join them soon? We'd rather you hung around with us. (There you have it: this is just purely selfish reasoning!)

But we wish for you lives that are not only long but well-rounded, happy, and nourished.

Historian H. G. Wells is said to have commented in his diary, "I am sixty-five, and I am lonely."[1] Former U.N. General Secretary Dag Hammarskjold wrote essentially the same thing.[2]

---

1. Quoted in Donald N. Paulson, "How to Deal with Your Loneliness," *The Watchman-Examiner,* 8 August 1968, 494 (quoted in a pamphlet entitled "Loneliness" by Stephen Olford).

2. Ibid.

It's an age-old problem. In the fourth century B.C., Seneca is said to have cried, "Listen to me for a day—an hour—a moment! Lest I expire in my terrible wilderness, my lonely silence! O God, is there no one to listen?"

God said it in the beginning: "It is not good for the man to be alone" (Gen. 2:18).

You men die sooner than we do. And the research is showing it's because of the sickening aloneness-environment in which most of you—why?!—choose to live. When you dear men try to be tough, unsentimental, objective, striving, achieving, and unexpressive—you're going to be unhappier and you're going to die sooner.

What's the point?

Those who study the situation tell us you have as many innate feelings as we women do. That means you have more secrets.

That means the people around you are threats to invasions of your privacy, so you stay more tense.

It means you must continually keep your guard up—and that's stressful, exhausting work.

Sidney Jourard says that the man who hides and stays inaccessible to others becomes "an immensely fertile 'garden' in which viruses and germs proliferate like jungle vegetation."[3] When you insist on staying closed, you actually become opened—opened to every sickness attack, every mental, emotional, and physical debilitation.

> If love is a factor that promotes life, then handicap at love, a male characteristic, seems to be another lethal aspect of the male role.[4]

Is the armor you wear your pride? I know some of you never take it off—not even at night in bed with your wives.

---

3. *The Transparent Self* (New York: Van Nostrand Co., 1971), 41.

4. Ibid., 40.

If my husband wore a full array of armor in bed, how could I hug him? And how could I know what Ray Ortlund really looks like if I never saw him naked?

Alas for all you men who stay armor-clad twenty-four hours a day! Certainly your wives can't seek to meet your needs; they have no idea what they are. Listen, your wives have a hard enough time even staying in love with you; it's unnatural to love a stranger.

We women mourn.

We feel cheated.

We weep, before your funerals ever happen!

There you are, encased in your stupid armor, afraid to undress. And so you shut yourselves in to your loneliness and despair . . .

And, too soon, to your deaths.

26 Building relational muscles

Anne continues . . .

I have a Filipino friend whose husband is a leading Christian in the Far East. We've often met in Manila, so when she came to California we went out to lunch together.

"Tell me, Maria," I said, leaning across my salad and roll and feeling chummy, "you're on both sides of the Pacific a lot; you know us well. So how would you compare American culture with Filipino culture?"

Maria burst out without any hesitation, "Oh, I feel so sorry for you! You people are so busy and so separate—you actually have to *make appointments* to see each other! We can drop in on each other anytime. We're close; everybody's family. We don't have to look right or have the house just so; we just need to be together. Everybody feels that way."

I've heard that Mother Teresa says the same thing about Westerners: "I am sorry for you! You have material things, but you're so poverty-stricken in relationships! In India we poor know each other. We network, we support each other, we lean on each other."

I remember when Merle, a financial tycoon, received Jesus and soon after, joined Ray's current small group. He couldn't believe it! For the first time in his half-century of life, Merle's feelings began to wake up. When he talked about the Lord, constantly, he got weepy, constantly. He couldn't get over what it meant to love other men, even hug other men, have true friends and share his emotions.

Merle said, "I've always thought of other men as competitors to 'do in' and climb over. I had no idea I was supposed to love any of them; I didn't know such a thing was even possible!"

Says British author Malcolm Muggeridge in his book *Something Beautiful for God,*

> The biggest disease today is not leprosy or tuberculosis, but rather the feeling of being unwanted, uncared for and deserted by everybody.[1]

It started a long time ago. The first couple sinned—and turned wimpy. So they put on dumb fig leaves to hide from each other. Then they crouched behind trees—what a joke—to hide from God.

The first Adam got us into trouble—but the second Adam, Jesus Christ, offers us a way out: "Love the Lord your God with all your heart and with all your soul and with all your strength and with all your mind," and, "Love your neighbor as yourself."

Open up your heart! Risk! Be vulnerable! Give yourself away—to God and others!

And one of His final commands just before the cross was, "A new command I give you: Love one another. As I have loved you, so you must love one another" (John 13:34).

There are many elaborations on the theme in the rest of the New Testament:

---

1. (New York: Ballentine Books, 1971), 55.

Love must be sincere [without deceit, pretense, or hypocrisy, truthful, genuine, real]. . . . Be devoted to one another in brotherly love. Honor one another above yourselves. . . . Share with God's people who are in need; practice hospitality.

Bless those who persecute you; bless and do not curse. Rejoice with those who rejoice; mourn with those who mourn. Live in harmony with one another. Do not be proud, but be willing to associate with people of low position. Do not be conceited.

Do not repay anyone evil for evil. Be careful to do what is right in the eyes of everybody. If it is possible, as far as it depends on you, live at peace with everyone. Do not take revenge, my friends, but leave room for God's wrath, for it is written: "It is mine to avenge; I will repay," says the Lord. On the contrary:

"If your enemy is hungry, feed him;
      if he is thirsty, give him something to drink.
In doing this, you will heap burning coals
      on his head."
Do not be overcome by evil, but overcome evil
      with good (Rom. 12:9–21).

Jump in. The water's fine.

I hear that most people have a pool of 500 to 2,500 acquaintances. Ray and I must be at the upper end. (How did it happen? We're just ordinary people.) We send out about 1,100 Christmas cards, most to couples and families.

A few hundred of these we've discipled over the years in small groups of six to eight, starting a new group once a year.

We each have our current small groups now, plus an even closer inner circle of immediate family (twenty-three at the moment), board members (very special) of our ministry, our much-loved secretary-assistant and her immediate family, and several hand-picked friends (a few couples, plus some girlfriends for me and close guys for Ray). With our traveling ministry, it keeps us jumpin' to keep up with all the family birthday parties and holiday times plus lunches and other social occasions with all our buddies.

Think about Jesus' network. There were more friendships than we know: The Son of Man came eating and drinking, and you say, "Here is a glutton and a drunkard, a friend of tax collectors and 'sinners'" (Luke 7:34).

He had levels of friendship: Nicodemus, Joseph of Arimathea, and probably hundreds of "disciples" (Luke 6:13, 17). Drawing closer, there were the women who traveled with Jesus and the apostles, ministering to their daily needs (Luke 8:1–3). Then there was a special family of three, Lazarus, Martha, and Mary. And the Twelve (Luke 6:14–16)—and out of the Twelve, particularly three: Peter, James, and John. And out of the three, maybe His dearest friend was John (John 13:23; 19:26, 27). We can believe, behind the scenes, it took a lot of time to keep up with His friends.

Or Paul. Here was a strong, tough, intellectual he-man survivor:

> I have worked much harder [than others in ministry], been in prison more frequently, been flogged more severely, and been exposed to death again and again. Five times I received from the Jews the forty lashes minus one. Three times I was beaten with rods, once I was stoned, three times I was shipwrecked, I spent a night and a day in the open sea, I have been constantly on the move. . . . [Paul covered most of the Middle East on foot.]
>
> I have labored and toiled and often gone without sleep; I have known hunger and thirst and have often gone without food; I have been cold and naked. Besides everything else, I face daily the pressure of my concern for all the churches . . . (2 Cor. 11:23–28).

And yet—or maybe *because of* his suffering—what a capacity for love! He wept when he hugged and kissed the Ephesian elders (Acts 20:36, 37). He had deep friendships with Luke, Timothy, and Apollos. He freely gave people his time, his emotions, himself:

> We loved you so much that we were delighted to share with you not only the gospel of God but our lives as well, because you had become so dear to us (1 Thess. 2:8).

This mode of functioning beats ego.

It beats getting lost in T.V. and the paper.

It beats being stranded, unknown, on Cliché Island, jabbering news-weather-sports.

27 How-to's for small groups that get you somewhere

<u>Ray writes</u> . . .

A few years ago, I'd been out of pastoring Lake Avenue Congregational Church for maybe five years. Their new pastor had taken over and he was doing great. Perfect, in fact. He was getting stuff done that I couldn't bring about in my twenty years of ministering there. I was glad for his success.

But I hurt.

I showed up at the regular meeting of my small group of young pastors—"of whom the world is not worthy," I tell Anne. They are pure gold.

"Guys," I said, "I need your prayers. I hate to admit it, but I'm just plain jealous of my successor at Lake. I don't like it, but I can't shake all these thoughts and feelings."

They prayed for me. (How I love those men!) And Christ washed out of my heart all the negatives, and He put me at rest.

Later, one of the fellows told me, "I was so helped when you opened your heart." And not long after, we all wept together over the daughter of one of the group who was going through heartbreak. His tears were ours as we gathered around him and prayed for her.

There's no substitute for groups where in reality you can "carry each other's burdens" (Gal. 6:2).

I remember how, for me, it all started. I'd been pastoring Lake Avenue for maybe ten years, and I was out of gas. I called together some good men who were particularly close to me, and I told them what I was going through.

I said, "Guys, I just can't do this job anymore by myself. I feel 'hung out to dry'—all alone in this ministry. I need some men around me who will love me, encourage me, straighten me out where I need it, and help me walk with God.

"Will you meet with me once a week for two hours? Could we commit our hearts to each other? I'd like to encourage you, too. It'd be a two-way street."

The men discussed it a bit, and they said they were terribly busy. Each one had some excuse. I began to think, *What I have in my hands is a lead balloon.*

Finally Ted Engstrom, bless him, took charge, his chin quivering. "Look," he said, "this isn't a discussion time; this is an altar call. Are you willing? Are you?" And he went around the circle one at a time. Each man said yes.

For a year and a half we gave our hearts to Christ and to each other in a special way. And it was the beginning of a whole new thing in their lives and in mine. I began to open my heart to men who loved me. I began to share failures and successes, sorrows and joys. It wasn't easy at first to be vulnerable—believe me—but I started down an exciting road that's been crucial to my life ever since.

Jesus Himself set the pattern for us. About a year and a half into His three-year ministry He asked twelve men to be His small group, and He entered into a new and deep relationship with these twelve (Mark 3:13–14).

It meant a significant change in His lifestyle. Almost everywhere that He went, they went. The first half of His public ministry He'd spent largely with crowds; but now He spent more and more significant time with just these few.

Then came the cross and resurrection, and soon He would leave them. Now what?

Jesus gathered them together one last time, and He said,

> Go and make disciples of all nations, baptizing
> them in the name of the Father and of the Son and of
> the Holy Spirit, and teaching them to obey everything
> I have commanded you. And surely I will be with you
> always . . . (Matt. 28:19–20).

The men did just that. Acts 2:41 and following shows how they baptized and taught new converts, meeting in large groups at the temple and in small groups in homes (Acts 2:46–47). And the new plan was so successful, Christianity exploded into action. Intimacy brings health, and health brings growth!

Here are some guidelines for meeting in a small group:

1. Pray first about those who should be in your group; don't just rush into it. Jesus prayed before He picked; there's your example (Luke 6:12–13).

2. Five to seven men is about right. In my experience, more than that doesn't allow enough time for all to participate.

3. Keep the group Christ-centered by beginning with some prayer and worship. And always go to the Bible together, even though it's important not to let it become just an impersonal Bible discussion group.

   (*The Transparent Self* comments on this danger, "It is possible to be involved in a social group . . . for years and years, playing one's roles nicely with the other members—and never getting to know the persons who are playing the

other roles."[1] Plenty of "home Bible study groups"
are like this.)

4. Meet weekly at a time when there'll be no inter-
   ruptions. Not much is happening at 6:00 A.M.! Start
   promptly and end promptly; don't trap busy guys.

5. Make a covenant together of your reasonable and
   prayed-for expectations, and "sign it in blood":
   "This isn't merely a meeting we go to but a relationship we're in."

6. Decide, at the start, on your cutoff time. Anne's
   groups meet September to June. Mine usually
   meet January to December; men take longer to get
   in there!

7. Swear to keep all confidences, and if anyone
   breaks the rule he must be confronted. For the
   group it will be a growing experience. Trust means
   everything.

My groups tend to meet for an hour and ten minutes in the
morning, and then those who can, go on to breakfast together.
Most do, and we have a wonderful time going deeper.

When we meet we seek to do five things: worship, get into
the Word, share what's happening in our lives, pray for each other,
and be accountable to each other. I may lead, or by prearrange-
ment another may lead.

Once a year we have an overnight retreat, and occasionally
we have potlucks with our wives joining in. We have assignments
each time, maybe in Scripture memory or something to sharpen
our lifestyles—dates with our wives or one-on-one times with the
kids, et cetera. There are plenty of ideas for variety in Anne's
book *Discipling One Another,* published by Word.

---

1. Sidney Jourard, *The Transparent Self* (New York: Van Nostrand Co.,
1971), 31.

God tells us to "carry each other's burdens":

Brothers, if someone is caught in a sin, you who
are spiritual should restore him gently. But watch yourself, or you also may be tempted (Gal. 6:1).

We're told to "look not only to [our] own interests, but also
to the interests of others" (Phil. 2:4).
We're told to love one another "more and more" (1 Thess.
4:9–10).

Two are better than one,
  because they have a good return for their work.
If one falls down,
  his friend can help him up.
But pity the man who falls
  and has no one to help him up (Eccles. 4:9–10)!

Faithful are the wounds of a friend (Prov. 27:6).

As iron sharpens iron,
  so one man sharpens another (Prov. 27:17).

God Himself is not a loner. He's a Trinity. He's both "He"
and "They"; fellowship is built in.
He never intended for a man to be a loner, either. Like God
Himself, you need to love and be deeply loved, to know and be
deeply known, to be caring and to be beautifully cared for.
Love God! And then love others!

28 Mentoring and being mentored

Ray again . . .

Everyone's talking fathering these days. Books are out which imply that father-exposure is more strategic than mother-exposure; that dads need to be up to their eyeballs in diaper-changing and Little League; and that if you got little of Dad in your own life you're probably made of very inferior material.

There's some sobering truth here. Seventy per cent of all juveniles in state reformatories in America come from fatherless homes![1]

But the Bible gives you balanced perspective on fathering, with remedies, solutions, and hope. It implies, for instance, that if you were poorly fathered, you don't need to whine over your past: Timothy's father was apparently a non-Christian Greek who was mostly off the scene, but his grandmother and mother's input was enough to turn out a spiritual great (2 Tim. 1:15).

Furthermore, at creation God took a fatherless woman out of a man. And at redemption He took a fatherless Man out of a woman.

---

1. "Bringing Up Father," *Time,* 28 June 1993, 55.

But, practically—what system did God put into place to make sure all believers get adequately fathered? Mentoring. The New Testament's full of it.

From the time that the apostle Paul first "adopted" young Timothy (Acts 16:1–4), Paul took over the role that Timothy's own dad had botched up. Later he wrote, "I have no one else like him. . . . Timothy has proved himself, because as a son with his father he has served with me in the work of the gospel" (Phil. 2:20–22).

When Paul wrote Timothy his first letter he called him "my true son in the faith" (1 Tim. 1:2). In the second letter he called him "my dear son" (2 Tim. 1:2). And he loved the relationship; in both letters he repeats "my son," "my son."

As a boy I, too, was "father-hungry." My traveling salesman dad was always gone except for weekends. Feeding his family of seven through all the depression years, maybe he had no choice.

Many men today—maybe most men—like me, got too little exposure to their fathers, and their souls are hungry to rediscover a "father" to make up for their lack.

But the Bible honors mentoring—or discipling—for everybody, regardless of their early experiences, because no physical father is an all-wise, all-righteous, perfect model. God wants to build into every believing man (as Titus 2:3–5 says He wants for the women, too) an extended family of surrogate Christian fathers, uncles, and grandfathers.

Besides, every man in Christ needs to be a "father," himself. Whether or not he ever produces physical children, he needs to give himself away, all his adult life, to shepherding others in the Christian walk (1 Pet. 5:24). He needs to for two reasons:

> **1. What it will do for him.** An Australian aborigine once said something like this: "I've been doing this initiation work with young men for forty years now, and I think I'm beginning to get it myself."[2]

---

2. As quoted by Robert Bly, *Iron John* (Redding, MA: Addison-Wesley, 1990), 233.

I can't tell you all I have learned about the Lord and about myself from discipling men!

2. What it will do for others. A young Christian Afghan told Anne and me when we met with him in darkness at midnight (we were living in his land during the grimmest days of Muslim oppression), "I don't dare even have a girlfriend, much less a wife; I know that soon they'll identify me and kill me. But, oh, before they get me, my goal is to replace myself with other Afghan believers!"

Every Monday morning that I'm in town I meet with a small group of young business men. This year's group is dynamite; they mean so much to me! (Frankly, probably I need them more than they need me; I need the fellowship of younger men with their interests and perspective.)

The first years I mentored I know I didn't do a great job—I was too soft and easy. Probably in my insecurity I was trying too hard to keep them comfortable and make them really *like* the group. But I've learned that the more you expect of the men, the better the group and the higher the morale.

A small group has to be solidly based on truth. Insincere chit-chat is not what they get up early one day a week for. So now we seek to "speak the truth in love" (Eph. 4:15).

I have them say the Scripture they've memorized to the whole group, or report on their homework, whatever it is. They may have memorized the names of the books of the Bible, or maybe they were to say one affirmation to their wives each day for the week—whatever it is they were to do, they report on it. "You can only ex-pect what you in-spect"!

Here's the agreement we men put together for this year's group:

1. To define the purpose, so all expectations are the same, we are seeking to fulfill the command of Christ to disciple one another and grow together in Him.

2. We will start and end on time. Consistent lateness leads to discouragement.

3. We will be committed to complete our assignments.

4. We will attend all meetings unless ill. Availability is essential for consistent growth together.

5. As God helps us, we will each plan to start our own discipling groups after we've completed this year.

6. We will each make notebooks, to keep notes on what we do and on one another's prayer requests for prayer during the week.

7. We will commit our hearts to each other: "In accordance with Jesus' plan in John 13:34 and 35, I promise to love you men this year with a selfless love, a serving love, an unconditional love, and a responsible love, the Holy Spirit being my helper."

Now and then, when you least expect it, small groups will suddenly see fireworks.

I remember when David came tramping into our meeting looking like black thunder. We asked what was wrong.

"It's our anniversary," said David, "and no way can I take Mary out tonight or get her anything. I'm dead broke."

Well, we had our meeting, and we prayed for David . . . Somehow when David went out to get in his car there was sixty bucks under his windshield wiper—ten from each brother.

Months later, one morning David came in and slapped a check down on the coffee table in the middle of us. "Guys," he said, "I just sold a building. This four thousand's the tithe on the profit, and you all are going to help me spend it."

So we all chipped in ideas on what missions were good or what situations were needy, and that morning we each fulfilled our own fantasy: we "spent" four thousand bucks for the Lord's work—with a lot of hootin' and hollerin'.

Besides that, the closeness will sometimes grow until it becomes unbelievably sweet. The Governing Board of the second church I pastored in upper New York State got like that. Together we'd steered a growing church, gone through a couple building campaigns, loved and prayed and cried together. When I left they gave me a plaque. On one side was "our verse":

> Seek ye first the kingdom of God and his righteousness, and all these things will be added unto you (Matt. 6:33).

The other side, to which they all signed their names, said this:

> There are many events that come to mind as we say good-bye now to you, our leader on the Governing Board and our brother in Christ in all things. We look back on missionary conferences and joint-board dinner meetings, planning meetings at First Pres., Bible Studies at the men's retreats at Camp Pinnacle on a sunny fall day, Faith Promise calling and covered dish suppers, ice cream socials and all church picnics—and each of them and many more had a place in God's plan for us. But the times of deepest fellowship for us as a group have been when we pushed back our chairs and knelt together before the throne of Jesus—and this is the fellowship which abides.
>
> We praise God for your faithful ministry to us in the Lord Jesus Christ, and as a Governing Board we pray His richest blessing on your continuing ministry.

Look—in your life, leave behind you a trail of men who are tigers, sold out to Jesus Christ—and who will turn around and reproduce other tigers!

Listen to Paul's plea:

> Oh, Timothy, my son, be strong with the strength Christ gives you. For you must teach others those things

you and many others have heard me speak about.
Teach these great truths to trustworthy men who will,
in turn, pass them on to others (2 Tim. 2:1–2, TLB).

That's how the world will be salted with Christ-like men
who live obedient, gracious, wise, happy, reproducing lives.
The world today needs men who are not for sale:

> Men who without reservation are committed for
> life to Jesus Christ;
> Men who will stand when the world around them
> goes crazy;
> Men who will tell the truth and look the world
> right in the eye;
> Men who will eat what they have earned and wear
> and drive what they can pay for;
> Men who are never afraid to say "no" . . . *or
> "yes"!*

If you're not now committed to a small group of guys, get
on your knees and tell God you're willing to get going.

Wrote Dietrich Bonhoeffer, "The gracious call of Jesus becomes a stern command. . . . Do not say you have not enough
faith. You will not have it so long as you persist in disobedience
and refuse to take the first step."[3]

---

3. *The Cost of Discipleship* (New York: Macmillan, 1939), 57.

29 Cultivating a special friend

Ray continues . . .

Says Pat Morley, "I think most men could recruit six pallbearers, but hardly anyone has a friend he can call at two A.M."[1]

How do you find somebody like that—whom you can go to, or somebody who also has the right to walk into your life at any time?

I actually stumbled into my first experience with this kind of open friendship. Years ago, every other Thursday afternoon pastors from our Pasadena area met together for a time in the Word and prayer. I was drawn particularly to one man in the group, and years later when the group dissolved, Lenox and I continued to meet to share our hearts and lives.

Remember that all deep friends were once casual acquaintances, people you just said "hi" to. "Show hospitality to strangers," says Hebrews 13:2. Do it not only because of their need, but because then a stranger becomes an acquaintance, and every acquaintance has the potential of becoming a friend.

---

1. *The Man in the Mirror* (Brentwood, TN: Wolgemuth and Hyatt, 1989), 117.

Acquaintances may move to becoming companions; that's stage two. You do things together—you're golfing buddies or you go to ball games . . . Your togetherness isn't threatening because you're occupied with something outside yourselves, not with each other. Most men stop there.

Here's a typical story. An attorney regularly played golf with a buddy, but then he had a heart attack and had surgery; he was laid up for quite a while.

Eventually he was well enough to get on the course again, and the two met as usual at the first tee.

"I hear you had a heart thing," said his buddy. "Are you better now?"

"Hey, I'm so good I can beat the pants off you."

Both laughed, and the game was on. That was it. The second man had made no attempt to contact his buddy when he was sick, and the other would share nothing. These two had superficially warm feelings for each other, but they had no thought of getting to be more than golf companions.

But with aggressive action you could probe for the possibility of stage three, developing a true friend—someone who shares a meaningful chunk of your life, and you, his.

A friend is one
To whom you can pour out
The contents of your heart,
Chaff and wheat together.

Whose gentle hands
Will take the chaff and wheat,
And with a gentle blow
Send the chaff away,
Never to be retrieved. . . .[2]

"What a friend we have in Jesus"! When we take Him at His word—that He's borne "all our sins and griefs," that He really has

---

2. Thank you, friend Carol Carpenter. Used by permission.

blown away the chaff—we can get the courage to move in to best-friend status. It's up to us: "Love is made complete among us so that we will have confidence. . . . Perfect love drives out fear" (1 John 4:17–18).

Now, it's a fact that true friendships turn out to be more than we really wanted them to be—more intense, more demanding. But that's just what God plans—to force us out of our self-centeredness, shallowness, and indifference.

Dale Carnegie comments on the typical self-occupied man, "His toothache means more to him than a famine in China that kills a million people. A boil on his neck interests him more than forty earthquakes in Africa."[3]

To become Christlike is a scary thing. It will wrest from you money, time, plans, emotions, interests. It will humble you and hurt you and remake you.

C. S. Lewis says somewhere, I'm sorry I don't remember where,

If you want to make sure of keeping [your] "self" intact, you must give your heart to no one, not even an animal. Wrap it carefully around with hobbies and little luxuries: avoid all entanglements; lock it up safe in the casket or coffin of your selfishness.

But in that casket—safe, dark, motionless, airless— it will change. It will not be broken; instead it will become unbreakable, impenetrable, irredeemable.

To become Christlike is scary—but to refuse to become Christlike is scarier.

So Anne and I are saying to you, break open your heart. Be willing for new possibilities.

---

3. *How to Win Friends and Influence People* (New York: Simon and Schuster, 1936), 93.

Often a true friendship develops through suffering.

Job was struggling. His typical male "friends" (?) stayed on the outside of him; they just sat around and philosophized, talking macho. "Miserable comforters are you all!" said Job (Job 16:2).

Moses was struggling, and his father-in-law became his friend (Exod. 18). Seeing his plight, Jethro could have thought, "Why get involved? Why make waves?" But he took his courage in his two hands and rescued Moses from a bad situation. The ensuing love-relationship resulted in Jethro's son accompanying Moses and Joshua into the Promised Land (Num. 10:29 ff.), and their descendants, the Kenites, being permanent dwellers in Israel (Judg. 1:16; 1 Chron. 2:55).

David was struggling under the threats of King Saul, and Jonathan, the crown prince, became his dear friend (1 Sam. 20:42), which also linked together their descendants (2 Sam. 9).

Because I'm in the ministry people come to me with their struggles, but usually that's different. I'm glad to counsel them as the Lord gives me wisdom, but that's not a basis for a friendship. We're on a one-way street: one gets nourished, the other gets depleted.

I think of only one case where a guy, Peter, came to me with a problem, and after the situation got back to health he began to take the initiative to encourage me, as well. I'm so grateful!

That's the way a true friendship must be—

We share our *mutual* woes,
Our *mutual* burdens bear.

I told you about my friend Lenox. After the pastors' prayer group was no longer functioning, the two of us kept meeting. What a man of integrity! Lenox is a thoughtful theologian, wise, strong, and open. He's a huge man, an ex-Princeton lineman, but he has great capacity to be either fierce or gentle. We laughed together, we cried together, always we prayed together. I would trust Lenox with my life, my wife, my children, my money—anything.

Then Lenox took a church halfway across the country. We phone, we write, we exchange books, and we travel great distances to see each other—but I knew I needed somebody else geographically close. Since Lenox, I can't ever again be without somebody I can love and be accountable to, eyeball to eyeball. I've stretched and I can't go back to the old shape.

(David was the same: when Jonathan was killed he couldn't go back to what he'd been before. He found Ahithophel—1 Chron. 27:33.)

Anne and I prayed.

So God opened a door . . . literally our local church door. There stood Ed, whom I'd known closely for years at Lake Avenue Church, but who'd recently moved to the beach area where Anne and I also now live.

"Ed," I said after we'd talked a bit, "I've been praying about my need for a special friend, to whom I can open my heart and life. I want to ask you if you'd be that, if you'll meet with me once a month for an unhurried time. I invite you to walk into my life wherever and whenever you want. I will be absolutely honest with you. I need that kind of accountability with a peer. And I would do the same with you. Think it over, and give me a call. Or let's meet and talk about it."

For several years, now, we've had a wonderful time. Ed's very different from Lenox, but I didn't need a duplicate. He has a keen mind and a tender heart. We're good safety nets for each other.

We love our unhurried lunches together. Our conversations run from our work to funny things that have happened, to our concerns for our kids, to feelings of inadequacy, to sins that have us by the throat, to "how do I handle this situation." We pray for each other. Every month I send Ed my schedule of responsibilities. When I rewrote the "affirmations" I say each day, I ran them by Ed. I know I could call Ed at two in the morning—without guilt—and he'd be there for me. I'd do the same for him.

You need a small group in your life, but you also need a special friend—one who knows you like a book, a confidant you utterly trust, for whom you're responsible and to whom you're accountable.

Moses had Joshua. Elijah had Elisha. That's what Jehoida the priest was to young King Joash. That's what the scholar Baruch was to the prophet Jeremiah. (What began as a business partnership turned into a romance!) And how about Peter and John, Paul and Timothy—olds with youngs who became peers in Christ.

God has given me more great close friends than I could count, men who've stood by me and encouraged me: in earlier days, Andy and Dale, who not once but twice, in the middle of the night, towed our broken-down car from Cape Cod to Schenectady . . .

Paul, a German hippie in Afghanistan I helped lead to Christ; we got so close that when I asked "Are you well?" Paul answered, "I am well if you are well . . ."

Ted, to whom I once confessed a great sin and he said, "Ray, it's all over; Christ's blood has covered it; God has forgotten it, now you do the same." He pronounced the grace of God on me . . .

Vince: "If I die, will you see that my wife and family are okay? . . ."

One of my very first good friends (though not as I now know good friends) was Don. We were teenagers who grew up in the same neighborhood in East Des Moines, Iowa. We hung out together and talked "oppy" and played pingpong. Don's parents were divorced. When I moved away to college, navy, and career, we lost touch.

Maybe thirty years later the phone rang in our home in Pasadena, California. I knew Don's voice right away, though it was muffled. He'd had a massive heart attack and was lying in intensive care. He'd told the nurse he had to make a phone call, and the nurse tracked down his old buddy Ray Ortlund and held the receiver to his ear and mouth.

"Ray," said Don, "I don't know, I could be dying, and, Ray, I needed to tell you about it. Thanks for leading me to Christ. Pray for me."

We had a brief but precious talk as Don connected with the Lord and knew he was ready for heaven. Then he had surgery, recovered, and we picked up our sweet friendship where we'd left off.

A great postscript to this story is that later his son moved to Pasadena. Here was this young man who looked like that Don I had known as a boy. He joined Lake Avenue Church, and I got to love him and, for my brother Don's sake, pour spiritual input into his young life. Blessing to the second generation! What a reward.

Now, a special friend is never the sum and total of all your Christianity. No one person can ever meet all your needs, and too-high expectations will suck too much juice out of another! Pursue with care, but don't push, don't force. Dick and Betty were our neighbors for fifteen years before suddenly they met Christ and became our dear friends.

And then there's the best friend, your wife. Oh, I hope yours is really a best friend, too!

The other Sunday Anne and I had gone to worship, and afterward we sat at lunch in a restaurant. As I looked across the table at her beautiful face, I thanked her for being my lovely friend. And I began to cry! I felt stupid but I couldn't help it; the tears just came out.

And as I write this and I think of special friends, I choke with gratitude to God. I wish I could embrace each one right now, and tell him how much he means to me.

Thank you, Lenox and Ted and Jim and dear Anne and Bud and Nels and John and Walt and . . .

PART VI

Your Love for Life

30

A basic mode for a man: good conversation, good manners

(Don't cut your toenails in front of company.)

<u>Anne begins</u> . . .

So what do you think—what does "manly" mean? At the beginning of this book Ray asked what's the style that makes you most genuinely masculine.

It really has nothing to do with tattoos, Harleys or headbands, and nothing to do, either, with short shorts and styled hair and working out.

A man grows into what he was really designed to be when he begins to love. His center of gravity shifts from himself to others. All others. Any others. A man and his *loves,* his *relationships:* That's what this book is all about, and that's what your *life* must be all about.

What is man's greatest fear? My suspicion is that it's not woman; what scares him most of all is himself.

Says Ray, every man is aware of his own maleness—of those inner masculine urges, those raging pressures which if not mastered will destroy him. He feels a heat inside himself which, when fanned, can break into flames and cause him to self-destruct.

His literal "salvation" is to say,

> Just as I am, though tossed about
> With many a conflict, many a doubt,
> Fightings and fears within, without,
> O Lamb of God, I come, I come!

Love God! That's your bottom line. Turn your attention from yourself, and come first to Him—not to your wife or anyone else. Come to Him, and let Him channel all that magnificent masculine energy into great, great causes, projects, and people. And when a man turns away from himself to love God and others, that's when he goes from *"man"* to *"gentle-man."* (Self-centeredness is basically ill-mannered, disgusting, gross.)

Notice the courtesy in 1 Corinthians 13's description of love; this has everything to do with a real man's style, his "mode of operations":

> Love is patient, love is kind, it does not envy, it does not boast, it is not proud. It is not rude, it is not self-seeking, it is not easily angered . . . (1 Cor. 13:4–5).

How is this going to work out practically, in your life?

You've seen guys push their way through a conversation like a fifteen-ton truck in traffic, ten times out of ten assuming the right of way. They probably have a bad case of "performance anxiety." Wait. Ask a question. Listen. Let your friend open up. Relax. Try comments like, "No kidding." "Boy, that's tough." "Wow! Amazing!" Watch his eyes. Take in what he says. Get genuinely interested in trying to figure out the man behind the words.

> Be devoted to one another in brotherly love.
> Honor one another above yourself. . . . Rejoice with
> those who rejoice; mourn with those who mourn
> (Rom. 12:10, 15).

Look at 1 Corinthians 13:5 in the Phillips paraphrase: "Love has good manners and does not pursue selfish advantage."

Once Ray didn't hire a man because his table manners were bad. He was sorry his mother hadn't taught him, but his manners also revealed that his center of gravity was himself. Maybe your mother didn't teach you, either; let me take over! No extra charge for a few basic tips, but if all this is obvious to you, forgive me:

At the table: Seat the ladies before you seat yourself.

Don't eat until everybody has his food; if there's a hostess, wait till she takes her first bite.

Don't push with your thumb.

Hold your fork or spoon between your fingers, not with your whole hand.

Don't chew with your mouth open.

Keep looking to see if you need to pass whatever dishes are in front of you.

Eat slowly. Keep your head up and make other people, not your food, your objects of attention.

Don't leave the table until the others do.

And a few other tips: Nothing on your head indoors unless you're orthodox Jewish.

Wait for women and children to go first through doors.

Always stand up when older people approach. Did you know that one's even in the Scriptures (Lev. 19:32)?

Watch out for women, children, older people, handicapped; offer them seats; if they're struggling, take care of them.

Mostly, *act to make other people happy.* Okay, don't say nobody ever told you.

Let's take another look at Jesus Christ, the Lord, to catch His style. Here's a real man, the model man, in action. Jesus

Had a wonderful conversation with a low-class Samaritan woman (John 3).

Welcomed a top-dog legislator for an evening ap-
pointment (John 3).
Touched lepers (Luke 5:13).
Had dinner at the home of wealthy Matthew
(Matt. 9:10).
Took kids in His arms (Mark 10:16).

He was always reaching outside of Himself, always loving.
He died to redeem us because He loves us. He rose again to give
us resurrection life, because He loves us.
Now, there's a Man.

31 Is it too late to go for the gold?

<u>Ray writes</u> . . .

The world is full of men who think it's too late. They feel defeated over one sin or many sins in their past that they think disqualified them. They think they don't have a right to be really happy, or see any kind of glory in their lives.

David, the great leader of men, civilian and military administrator, poet, musician, and a man after God's own heart, chose to commit adultery and then murder. You know the story; everybody remembers David's sin!

But first to Nathan the prophet, and then to God, David took his courage in his two hands and admitted the whole mess. With all the personal pain and embarrassment which a big shot would know to admit he'd fallen so far—knowing the news would soon race over his whole kingdom—David simply bowed his head and said, "I have sinned against the Lord" (2 Sam. 12:13).

No baloney about "I was framed . . ." "It happened because I just weakened a little at the wrong moment . . ." "Well, she was right there in broad daylight, brazenly washing herself . . ."

161

Just "I have sinned."

Weakness alibis. Weakness denies being wrong, being inferior. Weakness daydreams, Walter Mitty style, but rejects hard facts. Weakness goes through life excusing itself, justifying itself, explaining itself. Weakness whines. Weakness is tangled up in sin, so weakness is a wimp.

God never intended for anyone to wallow around in regrets. Nowhere, nowhere does His Word allow victimization or past abuses to excuse the present. That's what His forgiveness is all about, and it's any man's for the taking!

What God is into is strength, dignity, victory, and joy for all His children, and it all comes the same way: through understanding and personally receiving His grace.

> Amazing grace! How sweet the sound
> That saved a wretch like me!

God's kind of manhood is strong, and any man of His can be realistic about his sin and have the courage to stoop in total confession. David prayed,

> I know my transgressions,
>   and my sin is ever before me.
> Against you, you only, have I sinned
>   and done what is evil in your sight. . . .
> Surely you desire truth in the inner parts . . .
>   (Ps. 51:3–4, 6).

Then he had the confidence in God's grace to pray,

> Create in me a pure heart, O God,
>   and renew a steadfast spirit within me. . . .
> Restore in me the joy of your salvation (Ps. 51:10, 12).

Whatever your past, God can do the same for you. Will there still be scars? You bet. Your scars will remind you not to do it again.

But there are permanent scars on Christ, on His hands and feet and sides (John 20:25–28), to remind us all of this fact: "God made him who had no sin to be sin for us, so that in him we might become the righteousness of God" (2 Cor. 5:21).

If you've accepted Christ as your Savior—theology is emitting another roar!—*you have become the very righteousness of God.* In yourself, in your very being! That's how total is your transformation.

And now, what happens with your day-to-day sins—maybe even (God forbid) a whopper?

If we claim to be without sin, we deceive ourselves and the truth is not in us. If we confess our sins, he is faithful and just and will forgive us our sins and purify us from all unrighteousness (1 John 1:8–9).

So as soon as you're aware of sin, jump on it and confess it. Keep short accounts with God. And when you confess what little you're aware of (and we are all worse than we know) God purifies us from all—did you get that?—*all* unrighteousness. Everything else that you're not aware of, God forgives as well.

That's God grace! He loves your humility, your willingness to admit your sin, and He will keep you squeaky-clean.

Now you can hold up your head. Fill your lungs with air. Love life! Love your own life, God's specific gift to you! Love God!

"I press on," wrote Paul, who in past days had chased, caught, and persecuted Christians and only God knows what else—

Forgetting what is behind and straining toward what is ahead, I press toward the goal to win the prize for which God has called me heavenward in Christ Jesus (Phil. 3:12–14).

Go for the gold, my friend! God Himself is cheering you on, all the way.

All Christ gives, He gives with power. Every blessing He bestows, every promise He fulfills, every grace
He works—all, all is to be with power. Everything that
comes from this Jesus on the throne of power is to bear
the stamp of power.[1]

Look, I know what I'm talking about. My life, my past—how
I regret some of that! But "by the grace of God I am what I am,"
in the dignity and productivity and joy of living for Him.

I can't get over God's mercies. I often pray, "Lord, You've
really done a number on me! I'm not that great. I know all too
well what a jerk I've been—but, my, Lord, You're so kind and gracious, I have a wonderful life. I ought to be booted in the pants;
it's hell that I deserve; but You've redeemed me and forgiven me
and hugged me in Christ!"

I said it to Anne just yesterday: "I'm a happy man. If it should
all end right now, sing a hymn of praise! It's been a wonderful jour-
ney." Because I know I'm totally forgiven, I am really loving life.

God's grace. Make it your personal logo.

---

1. Andrew Murray. Location of source unknown

32 The glory of fatigue

Ray again . . .

    I heard the president of Cal Tech speak one time about education. He said that the world should have many schools that are good, even fine. But he said there should be a few that are true way-show-ers, pacesetters, who influence the others toward the best.

    The same is true about men.

    So what kind of man do you choose to be?

    You may be saying, "Look, I'm tired. Get off my back. I live at a crazy pace already; I can't *do* any more, I can't *be* any more. Gimme a break."

    Two comments.

    Probably you need to cut out some fat. As Anne says, "Eliminate and concentrate." Subtract from your schedule some of the clutter, the baloney, the stuff that's inconsequential.

    Here's what 1 Corinthians says in *The Living Bible:*

> In a race, everyone runs, but only one gets the
> prize. So run your race to win. To win the contest you

must deny yourselves many things that would keep
you from doing your best.

An athlete goes to all this trouble just to win a
blue ribbon or a silver cup, but we do it for a heavenly
reward that never disappears.

So I run straight to the goal with purpose in every step. I fight to win. I'm not just shadow-boxing or
playing around (1 Cor. 9:24–26 TLB).

My little book *Lord, Make My Life a Miracle* ends with these
words:

> Your danger and mine is not that we become crimi-
> nals, but rather that we become respectable, decent,
> commonplace, mediocre Christians. The twentieth-
> century temptations that really sap our spiritual power
> are the television, banana cream pie, the easy chair, and
> the credit card. The Christian wins or loses in those
> seemingly innocent little moments of decision.
> Lord, make my life a miracle![1]

Second comment.

What's wrong with getting tired? John, chapter 4, says that
a whole village got converted after Jesus talked to one of their
women when He sat down by their well *because He was tired.*
Out of fatigue, glory! Hey, being tired is okay!

Oswald Sanders says "the world is run by tired people."[2] Most
souls are won for Christ by tired Christians. The best sermons are
preached by tired preachers. The best youth camps are run by
exhausted youth ministers. The world is being evangelized by tired
missionaries. Tired executives run Christian organizations.[3]

1. (Ventura, CA: Regal Books, 1974), 151.

2. Oswald Sanders, *Spiritual Leadership* (Chicago: Moody Press, 1967), 108.

3. Thoughts taken from Kent Hughes, *Behold the Lamb* (Wheaton, IL:
Victor Press, 1984), 66.

Look—rest and recreation can't be top priorities in your life. Nowhere in the Bible are you told to slow down and take it easy; you're to press on.

> Let nothing move you. Always give yourselves fully to the work of the Lord, because you know that your labor in the Lord is not in vain (1 Cor. 15:58).

Expect to get tired, and then to be asked to give some more. (When the apostles were so busy they didn't even have time to eat, Jesus said, "Come with Me by yourselves to a quiet place and get some rest"—and immediately five thousand people arrived to be taught and then fed! . . . That's Mark 6:30–44.)

God isn't your servant, you are His. He's more interested in your Christ-likeness than your convenience. You can choose to play it safe, avoid hard work and troubles and tough situations, or you can "play the man"—and enjoy victories and rewards that others will never know.

The word today is, "Give yourself space. Don't let others encroach on your 'boundaries.' Save yourself, serve yourself." God says, "If you cling to your life you will lose it; but if you give it up for me, you will save it" (Matt. 10:39, TLB).

Great athletes today have a term they call "playing hurt." You're in pain, you play anyway. Shannon Miller, young champion gymnast has, at this writing, had a sore back for seventeen months. She's just won another world title.

I recently had a letter from my dear friend Doug, head of an important mission organization. From Singapore he had phoned his Jeanie, five months pregnant, and learned that their baby had just died in her womb. Catching the next flight home, Doug arrived at the hospital three hours before little Taylor Douglas was delivered, "his tiny body perfectly formed," says Doug.

Ten-year-old Judson, grieving, wrote his little brother a letter:

Dear Taylor,
I wish you could still be alive. I wish I could have seen you. I was looking forward to having a baby brother.

I was looking forward to coming home after school each day and seeing my little brother. I was looking forward to watching you grow up. I bet we would have been best buds. I love you, Taylor, and I look forward to seeing you in heaven.

Love, your brother—Judd

Writes Doug,

It is our desire that we will be able to redirect the love, time and energy that we would have invested in another child to others whom God will bring into our lives, and to the work of sharing the love of Christ at home, in Japan and throughout Asia in the years to come.

In a few days we will resume our work and our travels. . . .

Doug has learned to play hurt.

33 Great plans, final purposes

<u>Ray continues</u> . . .

Listen to these words of a young Billy Graham, preached in 1952:

> The great problem in America is that we have an anemic and watered-down Christianity that has produced an anemic, watered-down, spineless Christian who is not willing to stand up and be counted on every issue.
>
> We must have a virile, dynamic, strong, aggressive Christian who lives Christ seven days a week and who is ready to die, if necessary, for his faith. We need Christians who are ethical, honest, gracious, courteous, bold, strong and devoted followers of the Lord Jesus Christ. . . .[1]

There is the exciting slam-bang quality of a young warrior in these words, and yet a remarkable similarity to the old warrior

---

1. "The Despair of Loneliness," a tract of the Billy Graham Evangelistic Association, Minneapolis, © 1952.

of today, whose message has never changed and whose spirit has never flagged.

But where are the young warriors to replace the older ones? The need is much greater than a generation ago.

Friend, love your privilege of being a man,
    love God,
    love your wife,
    love your children,
    love others in your life's circle,
and then, expand your heart to love some more:
Love this needy world!

The test of any civilization is how its people treat their weak, the ones with the least power and influence. The weak are defenseless—whether they're fresh and young, still in the womb, or wrinkled and old, lying in some tragic place. They can't fight back. They can't stand up for themselves.

And a measure of a strong man is the passion of his defense of the weak. God feels keenly about whether a man is like that or not (Prov. 14:31; 22:9, 22, 23; 29:7). He says,

> Speak up for those who cannot speak for them-
>   selves,
>   for the rights of all who are destitute.
> Speak up and judge fairly;
>   defend the rights of the poor and needy
>   (Prov. 31:8–9).

When Jesus said, "Love your neighbor as yourself," He called it the law of greatest importance excepting only the law to love God Himself (Luke 10:27). When innocent people are threatened or mistreated, a society of wimps chooses to become the priests and Levites who look away and cross to the other side of the road. They "don't want to get involved."

Listen to God's scathing condemnation of such people:

> On the day you stood aloof
>   while strangers [abused your brothers],

> you were like one of them. . . .
> The day of the Lord is near. . . .
> As you have done, it will be done to you
> (Obad. 1:11, 15).

Christianity itself has shifted into the let's-not-offend mode of wimps. When did you last sing "Onward, Christian Soldiers" or "Fight the Good Fight" or "Soldiers of Christ, Arise" or "Am I a Soldier of the Cross?" or "Sound the Battle Cry"?

Enemies are all around us—racism (Luke 10:27), paper crimes (Heb. 2:6–11), drugs and alcohol (Prov. 20:1, Eph. 5:19), homosexuality (1 Cor. 6:9–10), abortions (Ps. 139:13–16; Jer. 1:4, 5; Luke 1:15, 41, 44), divorce (Mal. 2:14–16). Against these threats and many more, few Christians raise the sword. We whimper the favorite slogan of the wimps: "Let's not be controversial." We succumb to Satan's most lethal and pervasive lie, "Every person has a right to make up his own mind." So evil's death-waves lap at our very feet, and we crouch there weakly babbling about "love" and "forgiveness"—invaded, helpless, confused.

And the longer we refuse to react and act, the more we become cold, feelingless, withdrawn, numb, shriveled, pitiable.

Just as a wimp can't fight *against*, neither can he fight *for*. He has no passion to battle for his marriage, his daughter's purity, his college son's stand on biblical truths.

So what does a wimp do with all that dragon-slayer energy which God strongly built into him? He pays other soldiers to do his fighting for him—on the football field or through T.V. boxing or blood-and-guts movies. Or worse, he spends that energy in wife beating, drug violence, child abuse, street gangs, murder.

Look—"spiritual warfare" isn't a seminar you take or a book you read, to ponder and discuss the good guys and the bad guys. In our day moral standards are collapsing, and battles on every hand are about to be lost—for want of men of God who will clamber up over the sweating bodies of advancing evil-doers and with all their might roar a thunderous "NO!!"

> God did not give us a spirit of fear, but of power
> and of love and of a sound mind (2 Tim. 1:7, KJV).

A wimp settles for "Thus saith the majority." But where are the righteous men who will cry, "Thus saith the Lord"?

Is there a new Jonathan, who will again set an example of courage to younger brothers watching him (1 Sam. 14:4–12)?

Is there a new Caleb, who will take mountains (Josh. 14:6–14)?

Is there a new Phineas, who will attack immorality (Num. 25:1–13)?

Is there a new Joash, who will defend the threatened innocent (Judg. 6:25–32)?

Is there a new John the Baptist, who will expose sin in high places (Matt. 14:3–4)?

> Rise up, O men of God,
>   Have done with lesser things:
> Give heart and soul and mind and strength
>   To serve the King of kings.
> Rise up, O men of God!
>   The church for you doth wait,
> Her strength unequal to her task;
>   Rise up, and make her great!

34 "Loose him, and let him go"

Ray and Anne together . . .

A committed man becomes a transformed man, says Romans 12:1, 2:

> I urge you, brothers, in view of God's mercy, to offer your bodies as living sacrifices, holy and pleasing to God—which is your spiritual worship. Do not conform any longer to the pattern of this world, but be transformed by the renewing of your mind.

He says, "I urge you."

It's your move.

"Offer your bodies as living sacrifices." Your physical body, your personality, your gifts and abilities, your strengths, your weaknesses, your past, your present, your future. Offer your Self.

"Do not conform." Don't be squeezed into anyone else's idea of what's right. God has in mind a special kind of masculine glory personally just for you.

"Be transformed." What will He make of you?

Mary and Martha once sent Jesus word that His special friend, their brother Lazarus, was dangerously sick. They needed Him fast! But what did Jesus do?

He stayed where he was two more days! (John 11:6)!

Think of the way Mary and Martha must have felt. Two days of silence. Why did Jesus wait?

Because His plan wasn't to heal a sick man, it was to raise a dead one. He wanted to display even greater power, and that's why He let more time pass. And that period of silence was the prelude to one of Jesus' greatest miracles.

Reading a book is a silent thing. As through it you reexamine your life—the shape you're in right now, your love for God, for your wife, your kids, others—what will happen next?

You could be stumbling into becoming a great man of God— not conformed but transformed.

Ask Him through this book to break you out of the straightjacket of your self-centeredness, caution, inhibitions, fears, lethargy.

Jesus' last (and best) words to Lazarus came after He'd given him back his life; He said, "Loose him, and let him go" (John 11:44 KJV).

Your world is waiting. So is God—but He won't wait forever.

Write us of your new decision.

Sincerely in Christ,

Ray and Anne Ortlund
4500 Campus Drive, Suite 662
Newport Beach, California 92660
U.S.A.

Questions for Reflection and Discussion

Part I

1. Jot down your own definition of "manly." Share it with your group, your wife, and/or a trusted friend.

2. What benefit can you see from meeting together with a group of Christian men?

3. What's your biggest alibi for not doing what God wants you to? How has God strengthened you by weakening you?

4. What do you *do?* How is it "for the Lord"?

5. Who are your five most spiritual greats? What do they teach you about serving God?

6. Outline your own prayers as "ACTS." Does this change the way you pray? How?

Part II

1. What idols can stand in the way of a man's love affair with God?

2. When was a time when you felt cut off from the Source? What did you or can you do about it?

3. How are you going to hold yourself accountable for getting close to God?

4. Can you let God plug a hole in your heart? Try asking Him.

5. Are there times when you can "feel God in your face"? Describe, to a trusted friend, how that feels.

Part III

1. What are some ways you can get to know your "echo of yourself," your wife?

2. When is the last time you found out something you didn't know about your wife? Or shared something with her she doesn't know about you? Do it.

3. How can you help your wife feel "side by side" with you?

4. When has the wimp factor led you to sin? Bottom line: What can you do about it?

5. "Leadership ain't easy." How can you meet the challenge?

Part IV

1. Who is God to you? How can you be more like His father-copy?

2. What are some concrete ways you can show your love for your children?

3. What are some tough situations you face as a family? How might dispensing grace work better than laying down the law? Under what circumstances, if any, would laying down the law be better?

4. What would you say to your daughters that reflects the benediction of God on your relationship with them?

5. What style are you transmitting to your son? Do you want to change it? Do you want to change the way you transmit it?

6. Think about some ways you can bless your household—daily and during times of crisis or to mark life's big events.

7. What do you need from your Father to help you stand as a father, sheltering your family against the world?

8. Who are your personal role models and heroes? How can you begin sharing them with your family?

Part V

1. What can you do to live so your woman won't "mourn and feel cheated?" Start today.

2. Who do you *really* talk to? What do you have to say?

3. If you're not in a small group, ask God for help to find one or begin one—soon. If you are, right now, thank God together for your group.

4. What are some changes you're willing to ask God to help you make so you're "not for sale"?

5. What can you do to begin to cultivate a special friend?

Part VI

1. Read 1 Corinthians 13 and ponder how love makes for considerate living. What verses or phrases here can you implement in your own life?

2. Read Psalm 51:1–7 and use it as a model for confessing your own sins. First, write your confession on paper, taking about five minutes of silent time. Then, if you're in a group, share what you can with the group.

3. How can you eliminate the unnecessary in your life and concentrate on the necessary?

4. Right now—today—what are some ways you can "rise up, O man of God," and fight for right?

5. What would you be like if you were "loosed and let go"?

Bibliography

Adler, Jerry: "Drums, Sweat and Tears" (*Newsweek Magazine*, June 24, 1991), pp. 46–51

Belz, Joel: "Lots of Muscle, Lots of Restraint," lead editorial (*World Magazine*, Box 2330, Ashville, NC 28802, Vol. 8, No. 11, July 17, 1993)

Bernikow, Louise: "Alone, Yearning for Companionship in America" (*New York Times Magazine*, Aug. 15, 1982)

Bly, Robert: *Iron John* (Addison-Wesley Pub. Co., 1990)

"Bringing Up Father," cover story (*New York Times Magazine*, June 28, 1993)

Carnegie, Dale: *How to Win Friends and Influence People* (New York: Simon and Schuster, Inc., 1936)

Crabb, Larry: *Men and Women: Enjoying the Difference* (Grand Rapids: Zondervan Publ., 1991)

Colson, Charles: *Against the Night* (Ann Arbor: Servant Publications, 1989)

Dalbey, Gordon: *Healing the Masculine Soul* (Dallas: Word Publishing, 1988)

Davis, Lorraine, ed.: "American Men: What Do They Want?" (*Vogue Magazine*, June, 1986), pp. 236–307

Dobson, James: *Dare to Discipline* (Tyndale House, Regal Books, 1970)

Dobson, James: *Straight Talk to Men and Their Wives* (Dallas: Word Publishing, 1980)

Dobson, James: *What Wives Wish Their Husbands Knew About Women* (Tyndale House Pub., 1975)

Foster, Timothy: *Dare to Lead* (Glendale, CA: Regal Books 1977)

Gilder, George: *Men and Marriage* (Pelican Publ. Co., 1101 Monroe St., Gretna, LA 70053, 1986)

Gilder, George: *Sexual Suicide* (Quadrangle/ The New York Times Book Company, N.Y., , N.Y., 1973)

Harley, Jr., Willard F.: *His Needs, Her Needs* (Old Tappan, NJ: Fleming H. Revell Co., 1986)

Hughes, Kent R.: *Behold the Lamb* (Wheaton, IL: Victor Press, 1984)

Hybels, William: "What Makes a Man?" (*Moody Monthly Magazine*, June 1990), p. 15 ff.

James, Edgar: "Digging Deeper" (*Moody Monthly Magazine*, June 1990)

Jourard, Sidney: *The Transparent Self* (NY: Van Nostrand Co., 1971)

Lewis, C. S.: *The Four Loves* (New York: Harcourt, Brace and World, 1960)

Levinson, Daniel J.: *The Seasons of a Man's Life* (NY: Ballantine Books, 1978)

Morley, Patrick: *The Man in the Mirror* (Brentwood, TN: Wolgemuth and Hyatt Publ., 1989)

Mylander, Charles: *Running the Red Lights* (Ventura, CA: Regal Books, 1986)

Packer, J. I.: *The Puritan Idea of Communion with God* (address in London at a conference for ministers sponsored by Westminster Chapel, 1959)

Peter, Lawrence J.: *Peter's Quotations* (NY: Bantam Books, 1977)

Piper, John and Grudem, Wayne, eds.: *Recovering Biblical Manhood and Womanhood* (Crossway Books, 1991)

Piper, John: *What's the Difference?* (The Council on Biblical Manhood and Womanhood, P.O. Box 1173, Wheaton, IL 60189, 1989)

Pullman, Russ: "The Legacy of Faithful Parents" (*Tabletalk Magazine*, July, 1992), P.O. Box 547500, Orlando, FL 32854

Richmond, Gary: "In Pursuit of Manhood" (*Psychology for Living Magazine*, June, 1991), pp. 7, 14

Rushdooney, Rousas John: *The Counsel of Chalcedon Magazine*, Aug.–Sept. 1989 (P.O. Box 888022, Atlanta, GA 30338)

Smith, David W.: *Men Without Friends* (Nashville: Thomas Nelson Publ., 1990).

Stewart, Edward C.: *American Cultural Patterns* (Intercultural Press, P.O. Box 768, Yarmouth, ME 04096, 1972)

Tawa, Renee: "Banging the Drum Warily," (*Los Angeles Daily News*, Oct. 1, 1991, *LA LIFE Magazine*), p. 5

"Wild Men and Wimps," *Esquire Magazine*, special issue, Oct. 1991 (1790 Broadway, N.Y., N.Y. 10019)

World Magazine column entitled "Briefs" June 20, 1992 (Box 2330, Ashville, NC 28802)

Ziglar, Zig: *Raising Positive Kids in a Negative World* (N.Y.: Ballantine Books, 1985)